NOBODY

NOBODY

The Story of Bert Williams

ANN CHARTERS

THE MACMILLAN COMPANY

COLLIER-MACMILLAN LIMITED, LONDON

This book is affectionately dedicated to Reva Brown, who also believed in a book about Bert Williams.

The Macmillan Company
866 Third Avenue, New York, N.Y. 10022
Collier-Macmillan Canada Ltd., Toronto, Ontario

Library of Congress Catalog Card Number:
69-20215

First Printing

Book design by Jean Hammons

Printed in the United States of America

ACKNOWLEDGMENTS

I have been helped by many people in the years that have been spent in this study of Bert Williams' life and times. Since unfortunately no relatives and only a few of his friends are now alive, the bulk of my research was in great part the result of the cooperation of the staff at the Schomberg Collection and the Theater Collection of the New York Public Library. The Negro Actors Guild of America, Howard University Library, Harvard University Library, Brown University Library, and the University of California at Berkeley Library have also contributed information. For their very illuminating personal reminiscenses, I am grateful to several men in the theatrical world who graciously shared with me their memories of Bert Williams as a performer and friend, especially Eubie Blake, Harrison Smith, and Leigh Whipper. Pat Cather, Reva Brown, and Jim Walsh generously supplied me with sheet music, film, and tapes of rare recordings. And for general encouragement and advice, I thank Rudi Blesh, Langston Hughes, and Samuel Charters.

Bert Williams has done more for the race than I have. He has smiled his way into people's hearts. I have been obliged to fight my way.

Booker T. Washington

The drama is that the Negro is in your midst, the comedy is that he survives, the tragedy is that he is black.

Bob Cole

CONTENTS

THE FUNNIEST MAN I EVER SAW

THE LIFE of the Negro comedian Bert Williams is the story of a man neatly trapped by the prejudice and intolerance of his times. Racial prejudice has left its bitter stain over many aspects of the Negro's history in the United States, but it is perhaps nowhere so vividly illustrated as in its role in the development of the American popular theater. To some extent every immigrant group found its backgrounds ridiculed on the music hall stage, but for the Negro special conditions of prejudice, hostility, and ignorance insured a unique longevity to the stereotyped portrait. For over one hundred years the impression of the Negro as racially and socially inferior was fostered by legions of comedians in blackface. Originating in the white man's "imitations" of Negroes in nineteenth century minstrel shows, the caricature took such firm hold on the American imagination that audiences expected any man with dark skin, no matter what his background or inclinations, to be a "real coon." Even today a Negro actor is not free to appear on stage in whatever role he chooses, but when Bert Williams began his career in 1892, he found he had to conform to a theatrical convention that in many ways crippled his talent and limited his achievement. As a pioneer he was forced into a blackface role he detested, but in the theater the warmth of his comic genius was visible behind the make-up.

Audiences who saw Bert Williams in vaudeville or the Ziegfeld Follies before his death in 1922 still vividly remember him. Usually his appearance onstage was announced by a spotlight that caught the tentative wiggling of gloved fingers against the closed plush curtains. Hesitantly the hand followed the fingers, then an arm, a shoulder, and finally, with awkward reluctance, a tall man in a shabby dress suit pushed through the curtains and walked slowly to the front of the stage. The applause started before he reached the footlights, but the face behind the mask of blackface remained downcast. As if resigned to some inevitable and unending stroke of bad fortune, he shrugged his shoulders. With exaggerated care he searched his ragged coat pocket, pulled out a small leather notebook, and slowly turned the pages of the book until he found what he was looking for. Audiences settled into their seats expectantly when nodding in satisfaction, he began to half-sing, half-recite:

> *When life seems full of clouds and rain,*
> *And I am full of nothin' but pain,*
> *Who soothes my thumpin', bumpin' brain?*

He paused and shrugged with a sigh,

> *Nobody!*

> *When winter comes with snow and sleet,*
> *And me with hunger and cold feet,*
> *Who says "Here's twenty-five cents, go ahead and get something*
> *   to eat"?*

He shook his head sadly,

> *Nobody!*

Then he sang with a noisy wail,

> *I ain't never done nothin' to nobody,*
> *I ain't never got nothin' from nobody, no time.*
> *Until I get somethin' from somebody, some time,*
> *I'll never do nothin' for nobody, no time.*

> *When summer comes all cool and clear,*
> *And my friends see me drawin' near,*
> *Who says "Come in and have some beer"?*

A note of surprise in his voice,

> *Hum—Nobody!*

> *When I was in that railroad wreck*
> *And thought I'd cashed in my last check,*
> *Who took that engine off my neck?*

Suddenly resentful,

> *Not a soul!*

And again he lamented,

> *I ain't never done nothin' to nobody,*
> *I ain't never got nothin' from nobody, no time.*
> *Until I get somethin' from somebody, some time,*
> *I'll never do nothin' for nobody, no time.*

Williams first sang "Nobody" in 1905, and audiences responded so enthusiastically that he was forced to include it for the next seventeen years in nearly every stage appearance. It became his trademark, the statement of a hard-luck character who had done "nothin' for nobody, no time." Bert Williams was the first Negro entertainer in America to win the wholehearted admiration of white audiences, and in a *Variety* poll of 1953 which selected the names of the ten most important comedians in the history of the American popular theater, he was high on the list.

In addition to Williams' great popular appeal, the *Dictionary of American Biography* credits his "tact and character, as well as comic artistry," in helping the Negro achieve better conditions in the theater. His career ranged from the minstrel shows of the 1890's to the jazz revues of the 1920's, years in which Negro entertainers contributed a major share of the vitality of American popular culture. Occasionally Williams managed to transcend the racial stereotype his audiences expected of him, but for the most part he was trapped in a degrading role all his life. Off-stage a tall, light skinned man with marked poise and dignity, on-stage Williams became a shuffling, inept "nigger." He pulled a wig of kinky hair over his head, applied blackface make-up, and concealed his hands in gloves. Usually he wore a shabby dress suit and a pair of oversized, battered shoes, but sometimes for comic sketches in the Follies or for costume numbers in his own productions, he used other outfits: a redcap's clothes, a hotel clerk's uniform, once even a magnificent rooster costume. But usually he was in the old dress suit, working in front of the curtain while the sets were being changed behind him. The white collar that he wore was obviously false and unconnected to a shirt—no cuffs protruded at the wrists, just his gloves meeting the sleeves of a short black jacket. The jacket had once been a frock coat with long tails, but these had been cut off, and the jacket dipped strangely low in the back over trousers that exposed knobby ankles in wrinkled black socks disappearing into long, broad scuffed shoes. Williams' movements were slow and deliberate, his gestures clumsy and ineffectual, and with his bizarre costume they helped create a memorable stage character.

Bert Williams succeeded as a singer, dancer and comedian despite the fact that he had little natural singing ability and such poor co-ordination that he seemed to struggle with two left feet. After straining his voice through overuse in his early years he had to nurse it, as he said, "like a prize cat." What voice he had was a soft baritone with considerable roughness at the edges. In one of his later songs he even burlesqued his own singing. The song "Addio" by the Italian composer Tosti had swept the country, and its piercing chorus of

"Goodbye Forever! Goodbye Forever!"

was being sung by everyone from Caruso to school vocal recitalists. Williams began his version with a lilting patter listing all the things he knew about, from Ancient History to "Adam and Eve in the Garden of Eden"; ending with the plaintive question,

The thing I want to know
Is where did Tosti go
When he said—

Then in his best quavering baritone he went into the chorus of Tosti's song,

Goodbye Forever, Goodbye Forever,
I want to know where Tosti went
When he said Goodbye!

Williams' problem was to develop a singing style which wouldn't make his vocal limitations too obvious. What he evolved was a half-sung, half-recited approach to his material, presenting it as a comic sketch instead of a vocal performance. With subtle shifts of emphasis and an infallible sense of timing, he would momentarily create a real character. By his emphasis on important phrases, long pauses to suggest any ironic subtlety, and wry spoken "asides," he was usually able to get the audiences laughing so hard that they didn't pay close attention to the song. The pathetic figure he created with a tone of voice, a hesitant delivery, and a sorrowing manner was so distinctive that although his style has been imitated and his songs performed by other comedians, no one has ever approached his success with them.

As a dancer Williams had even less natural talent than he had as a singer, but despite this he became known for his dancing and usually included it in his stage appearances. He was tall, with long arms and legs, and rather than make an effort to learn some of the grace and style of an expert dancer like George Walker, his partner for many years, he emphasized his ungainliness. When Williams and Walker did a cakewalk, George would strut onto the stage with high step and arching toe, whirling through the dance. Bert would stumble after him, waving the sole of his shoe and flicking away a cigaret. For his exit after his solo numbers he worked out a step combining the worst features of the stage shuffle and the buck and wing. There are photographs of him getting off the stage with a harassed expression, looking something like a man who has just stumbled over a tree root while running sideways from a bee. Using his limitations as a singer to give his performances a wider comic range, he was also able to use his awkwardness as a dancer to give to his basic character, the black-face stereotype, a more individual identity.

The last difficulty Bert Williams faced working in the popular theater was the color of his skin. But unlike the limitations of his voice or his dancing abilities, this was the one difficulty he was never able to overcome. He was never, in his long years as a genuinely talented, highly paid comedian, able to leave off the burnt cork mask, the make-up he hated. W. C. Fields, who worked with him in the Follies and became his close friend, once remarked:

> *Bert Williams is the funniest man I ever saw, and the saddest man I ever knew.*

Regardless of his triumph in the theater, Williams was never exempt from the experience of racial prejudice. He might be a top ranking star when he clowned with Eddie Cantor in the Follies or held the vaudeville spotlight at the Palace, but once off the stage and out of the theater he was a fair target for the full battery of jim-crow slights and humiliations. The ignominious hostility he encountered as a Negro first limited his professional achievement and ultimately also destroyed his chances for personal happiness. All his life he struggled to adjust to intolerable situations; his triumph is that despite little encouragement he developed his unique comic gifts into an expression of considerable artistry. Possessing imperturbable personal dignity, he tried to rise above his situation, as when he said to an interviewer:

*People ask me if I would not give anything to be white. I answer . . .
most emphatically, "No!" How do I know what I might be if I were
a white man. I might be a sand-hog, burrowing away and losing my
health for $8 a day. I might be a street-car conductor at $12 or $15
a week. There is many a white man less fortunate and less well
equipped than I am. In truth, I have never been able to discover that
there was anything disgraceful in being a colored man. But I have
often found it inconvenient—in America.*

After Williams' success the door was to be opened for other Negro actors,
singers, dancers, and musicians. In his last years he saw Negro actors get more
opportunity in the American theater, as the star of Eugene O'Neill's play *The
Emperor Jones,* and as the highly acclaimed cast in the Broadway musical
Shuffle Along. But as a pioneer in hostile and intolerant times, Williams had
many moments of discouragement. Once when he doubted that he was reaching
his audience, he wrote a sketch satirizing their smug condescension:

First student of the Drama — *Now, you'll enjoy this fellow, he is
very funny. I remember the last time I saw him just before I left to
join the Lafayette Zouaves in 1869. He is always good. Perhaps you
don't fancy blackfaced comedians?*

Second student of the Drama — *My dear old chap, I am not so particular as all that. I can still laugh, I hope, without prejudice. These
sort of fellows can be very funny if they don't overstep the line of
probability. You know what I mean, if they are true to life.*

First student — *As I remember him (of course this is a long time ago,
when I was more susceptible to the theater perhaps and less exacting
in my standards), he had an unction, a* je ne sais quoi, *a mimicry that
was truly African.*

Second student — *African humor as I recall it in my college days
was chiefly delightful because it had that inimitable banjo flavor.
Does he play the banjo?*

First student — *Oh yes. Plays it with masterly humor. In fact, he
makes the banjo, a very inarticulate instrument, speak, actually speak!*

Second student — *Ah, that interests me. He must have a true spark,
then, in spite of being funny.*

First student — *I understand he is a very serious chap outside of his
profession. Reads by himself, don't you know, and all that.*

The truth is that Bert Williams really had the "true spark, then, in spite
of being funny." He is remembered today not only for his comic gifts, but also
as a man whose life is a drama of the struggle against the virulence of racial
prejudice. Unable to realize his highest ambitions, yet able to illuminate a degrading caricature with rare humanity, Bert Williams earned a place as one of
the most significant figures on the American popular stage.

$12 PER WEEK AND CAKES

I T WOULD probably have been just as easy for Bert Williams to try to grow wings and fly as it was for him to attempt escaping the blackface role of the stereotyped stage Negro. He began his career in 1892, less than thirty years after the Civil War had theoretically made it possible for a colored man in America to choose whatever occupation he wished, even a career in the theater. But if there was a theoretical freedom of choice guaranteed by the Emancipation Proclamation, the American popular stage offered a very restricted opportunity; in the nineteenth century, popular entertainment had developed little range or sophistication. As a seventeen year old boy setting out to earn his living as a singer, Williams had youth and courage working for him, but it was impossible for any one man, especially a light skinned Negro, to change the habits and prejudices of the nation.

The blackface role that Williams inherited had come out of the minstrel show, one of the earliest, hardiest, and most irrepressible entertainments on the American popular stage. Williams started his career when the comic theater was still a theater of types, caricatures without specific or individual identity. Using grotesque costumes and mannerisms, comedians noisily burlesqued not only nationalities like the stock figures of the Dutch, Irish and Italians who had settled in America, but also religions and races like the Jew and Negro. Williams could do little to change the situation; he found he had to conform to the prevailing image of the stage Negro. Because audiences would have ignored or hooted down a light skinned colored man presumptuous enough to perform without a heavy Southern accent, it was out of the question for a Negro to act in serious drama. For an entertainer who took on the stereotyped role, however, the situation had become so favorable that, as one old performer put it, "A colored man with a banjo would draw almost as big a crowd as an elephant in a circus."

Before the Civil War, the only Negro to achieve a name in the theater was the tragedian Ira Aldridge, who was born in America but left the country for a career in Europe. In the years of Reconstruction, the situation changed slowly, Negroes gradually being allowed a small place on the American stage (an 1889 *Harper's Magazine* article, "The Negro On The Stage," mentioned as a matter of course only white men masquerading in blackface). Ironically enough, the play *Uncle Tom's Cabin* opened the way for colored performers. This play and the minstrel shows were the two most popular stage entertainments of the 1860's and 1870's, and while at first Negroes were barred from the minstrel shows, they were allowed to appear in some of the smaller *Uncle Tom* companies in the roles of Cassie, Emmaline, Sambo, Gumbo, Pete, and Rastus. Until the 1880's, however, the characters Topsy and Uncle Tom were always played by white actors in blackface; Negroes were not judged sufficiently clever to memorize and deliver the long lines and important speeches.

After the Civil War, when all-Negro theatrical companies were formed, Negroes finally got a chance to imitate the white man's burlesque of their own presumed idiosyncrasies on the minstrel stage. As George Walker, Williams' stage partner, described the situation,

> *All that was expected of a colored performer was singing and dancing and a little story telling, but as for acting, no one credited a black person with the ability to act.*

> *Blackfaced white comedians used to make themselves look as ridiculous as they could when portraying a "darky" character. In their make-up they always had tremendously big red lips, and their costumes were frightfully exaggerated. The one fatal result of this to the colored performers was that they imitated the white performers in their make-up as "darkies." Nothing seemed more absurd than to see a colored man making himself ridiculous in order to portray himself.*

Although George Walker was painfully aware of the folly of Negro actors' imitations of the minstrel shows' degraded caricatures, both he and Bert Williams remained in the stereotyped blackface roles throughout their entire careers. In fact, Williams' performances were so widely imitated that he may be said to have prolonged the life of the caricature on the stage, however much he himself despised his role. Williams wanted to succeed in the popular theater, and if he had conscientiously refused to take on the stereotyped role he probably wouldn't have gotten anywhere. What might have been is a matter of conjecture, but what is certain is that by birth, environment, temperament, and natural inclination, he was totally unlike the caricatured "darkies." As Williams later admitted, he became a successful comedian only after he had come to see himself "as another person."

Like many famous theatrical people, there is a measure of confusion about Bert Williams' background. He contributed to the mystery himself by saying, "Nobody in America knows my real name and, if I can prevent it, nobody ever will. That was the only promise I made to my father." Various people claim to know when and where he was born, but no definite proof is ever advanced to support their theories. Leigh Whipper, a Negro actor who was in the Williams and Walker Company, said he heard from a reliable source that Williams was born in Riverside, California, on March 11, 1875, but the California State Department of Vital Statistics is unable to confirm this early date. Williams told a different story in the January, 1918, issue of the *American Magazine.*

My father was a Dane. He left Copenhagen some years ago and became Danish consul in Nassau. There he married my mother, who was half Spanish and half African. Her mother was brought over from Africa and destined for the Spanish Main, but thanks to an English frigate that intercepted the vessel she was brought in, she never reached her destination. She went to the British West Indies instead, where she married a Spanish cooper. Williams, of course, is obviously not a Danish name. Nobody in America knows my real name and, if I can prevent it, nobody ever will. . . .

This information was introduced by the magazine editor as coming from "A Negro, slightly over 40, who is one of the greatest and most successful comedians in the world." Probably the reporter who interviewed Williams became confused, however, for it would appear that it was the comedian's grandfather, rather than his father, who was the Danish consul. A few years later Williams told a friend that he was born on November 12, 1874, in Antigua, West Indies, a son of Fred and Julia Williams. His paternal grandfather had been Svend Eric "Williams," the Danish consul in Antigua, who married a West Indian girl who was three-quarters Spanish and one-quarter African. Their only child was Frederick Williams, Bert's father, who married a West Indian quadroon named Julia Moncuer, sister of an Episcopal clergyman of the Church of England in Antigua. Bert was christened Egbert Austin Williams.

This story is probably the one closest to the truth, and Williams' birthplace has generally been considered to be Antigua, the West Indies. It is very unlikely that, as he said in the *American Magazine,* his father was the Danish consul, since in September, 1909, Bert opened a pool hall for his father on Seventh Avenue in Harlem, and newspapers reported that "genial" Fred Williams soon made it a popular meeting place for the New York sporting set. Julia Williams, who survived her son's death, was a soft spoken lady with a distinct West Indian accent. Both parents were light skinned and very tall, and they passed these characteristics on to their son. Eubie Blake, a Negro vaudevillian, was impressed by Bert's parents when he met them in 1915: "They had big, big shoulders, like an Amazon's."

As a boy growing up in Antigua, Bert led a fairly comfortable life. The Williams family had some money, for his grandfather had retired from the consulship to operate a business exporting rum. Bert matured very quickly. He said that

I was always a big boy for my age. No matter what the age was, I never seemed able to catch up in years with the strides that my hulk made. I had that conspicuous feeling of being overgrown, in comparison to my playmates, that a Shepherd dog puppy might feel in a neighborhood of "pekes." As a young child I never seemed to have the surplus energy to expend; certainly none to squander, and I always got a great deal of fun out of observing the game, whatever it happened to be, and the various and varying human reactions upon the individuals who were active in it.

15

Even as a child, Bert was an introvert. He felt that in his early years he was

> . . . *storing away little character sketches that were always to serve me. In a way, as I consider this, I remind myself of an artist, now a well known illustrator, who was seated next to me at a supper party in New York one night. Somebody asked him if he could draw a lobster. He took out a pencil and drew a sketch on the table cloth. We all marvelled that this man could draw an anatomically perfect lobster from his memory, for we afterward compared his sketch with the photographic illustration in the encyclopedia. He said that he didn't know when he had seen a lobster, that he certainly never had drawn one before and that if the number of claws and the joints of them was correct, he thought it must be due to the dictation of his subconscious mind, which at some time had stored away the information for him.*
>
> *Truly, it seemed that I was and am still, constantly storing away dialects and little bits of mimicry, together with mental pictures.*

Despite his curiosity and gift of observation, Bert was only a mediocre student. His father recalled:

> *He studied just enough that he passed and his reports were good, but I am inclined to think that all the joy he ever got out of studying came from his own observations. Indeed he seemed delighted with each new achievement in mimicry and he developed this gift to a degree while only a child. We punished him for this at first, but soon discovered that punishment was of no use. I am mighty glad now, that the spark was there and that it developed in spite of us older folks who were so slow to understand and appreciate it.*

Bert Williams, Age 5

In 1885, the Williams family left the West Indies for California. They settled in Riverside, not far from Los Angeles. In the late 1880's Riverside was a small town, much more quiet than the busy seaport of Antigua. It was inland, very dry and dusty, with citrus and palm trees dominating the straggling lines of houses. Fred Williams took a job as a railroad conductor on the newly expanded Central Pacific lines. Like many Negroes from the British West Indies, the Williamses felt somewhat superior to their American neighbors, and although his father's job lacked much social prestige, Bert was raised to be conscious of the family's past distinction.

After his graduation from Riverside High School, Williams has said that he left his home in southern California to attend Stanford University, not far from San Francisco. He was unable to get financial assistance, however, and in the summer after his first semesters at the university, he tried to make some money. He and three friends he'd met at Stanford thought it would be easy to earn their tuition by touring in a wagon through the small California coastal towns, giving "entertainments." Traveling over the dirt roads to the towns of Felton, Santa Cruz, and Monterey, they clowned, sang, and strummed banjos for the unenthusiastic country audiences. When their college humor parodies and inept singing brought only meager applause and no tips, the students turned their wagon back to San Francisco. The company disbanded, Williams immediately burning his clothes, as he later explained, "for reasons that everybody will understand who has read of the experiences of the soldiers in the trenches."

Although the tour had been a financial failure, Williams did learn something from the experience. For the first time in his life he tried to be a professional entertainer, and he found he liked performing before audiences. Instead of returning to his parents in southern California, he hopefully approached the rambunctious theater world of San Francisco, a young singer with little more to offer than a slight banjo technique and a strong West Indian British accent. To make things worse, he was a tall, uncoordinated, and clumsy adolescent, and despite his light skin, a Negro.

In the beginning Bert Williams found San Franciscans as unresponsive to his talent as the Salinas ranchers had been. It wasn't that stage performances weren't appreciated in California. In the 1890's the theater was flourishing in San Francisco, and a Negro entertainer would be accepted—if his act were right —in a number of places. Although Negroes were rarely seen in the more pretentious concerts or stock company productions at the Grand Opera House, the Alcazar Theater, Stockwell's Theater, or Baldwin's Academy of Music, there was a lot of opportunity for individual performers in San Francisco variety bills. The earliest minstrel shows, music halls, and melodeons had featured variety acts, and several San Francisco theaters like the Orpheum and Billy Emerson's Bijou Opera House booked Negro singers, dancers, and comedians.

Theaters were no problem; the great obstacle was Bert's lack of experience. He had no specialty or large song repertoire, and he didn't want to make up as a clown. Also, since his background hadn't equipped him for the minstrel

17

stage, he couldn't immediately find a place there like so many other Negroes born and brought up in the South. After weeks of being refused by theater managers, he was forced to the conclusion that if he couldn't get a job on the stage, he'd begin his career on the lowest rung of the theatrical ladder. Like the other famous entertainers Eddie Cantor and Jimmy Durante, he got his first experience performing in saloons and restaurants.

Bert spent hour after hour in the smoky, poorly lit "free and easies" of the Barbary Coast, the tough waterfront neighborhood where the damp, foggy streets were cluttered with ramshackle wooden taverns, shabby boarding houses, outfitters' shops, and cheap restaurants selling oyster loaf, one of the town's specialties. Under the gas lights of East Street or Steward Street, the taverns catered to sailors on shore leave. Inside the crowded saloons waiters scurried to bring glasses of cheap lager beer and whiskey to impatient customers, and the quiet, soft-spoken young singer had to shout his songs to be heard above the din. Standing beside a noisy group of men at a table in the Hosker-Donken Saloon or Pat Ryan's Blue Shades Saloon, Williams tried to sing Irish ballads like "Little Annie Roonie" or nonsense songs like

> Doughnuts round,
> Weigh a pound,
> Drop them
> An' they shake the ground,

but he did not find much response on the Barbary Coast.

It was a long, hard winter. Bert tried everything. He took piano lessons from an unemployed "tickler" so he could play simple ragtime song accompaniments on the saloon uprights. For a month or two he even joined a group of Hawaiians who had a musical act in one of the cabarets, wearing a white blouse with a yellow lei around his neck in order to look as Hawaiian as possible.

Finally in the spring of 1893, Lew Johnson, a man who kept a barber shop in San Francisco, asked Williams if he wanted to be part of a little musical company that Johnson intended to take up along the California coast to play the lumber camps between San Francisco and Eureka. Almost desperate at this point, Bert joined the show. He earned $12 a week and "cakes, with an occasional chunk of pie," singing his songs and acting in the group's skits. Johnson's minstrel tours were an annual event in the isolated lumber camps hidden among the tall Sequoias and redwoods. The lumbermen were easily entertained and Bert found to his surprise that instead of the boos and cat-calls he had received with the Stanford students, he heard enthusiastic applause.

Lew Johnson's musical company returned to the city and disbanded, but Williams was so encouraged by this tour that he decided to try to move out of the cabarets and into an actual theater. During the past winter when he hadn't done well in the cafes with his banjo strumming, he had realized an unpleasant but inescapable truth. A Negro starting a career in popular entertainment faced only one choice in 1893: if he wanted audiences to watch him, he had to assume the "nigger" characterization. Working up an act that would appeal to theater managers, Williams began to practise the required stage dialect and posturing. But in an effort to partly escape the humiliating stereotype, he refused to wear the standard mask of burnt cork.

From the beginning, Bert Williams selected his theatrical personality with reluctance and deliberate detachment. He possessed none of the traits of the stage caricature popular in his time—neither the exaggerated Southern dialect nor the eccentric behavior that constituted the public's image of the tamed but only imperfectly Americanized African savage. Furthermore, with a background that had left him somewhat free from the experience of racial prejudice, he had few of the insecurities that many Negroes developed from the continued social pressure of being considered members of an inferior race. Instead, Williams' West Indian origin had given him a sense of superiority to the American Negro background that remained with him all his life. As a fellow performer said of him later, "Bert Williams was intelligent and he did not like Negroisms."

But after a valiant attempt to go his own way as a singer, Williams took on the conventional stage role because it seemed that this was the only way he could ever leave the cabarets. At first, in the early years of his study and analysis of the Negro comic character, he had to acquire the basic elements of his role. Setting out to become a minstrel man, he struggled with the "stage Negro" language, which he said "to me was just as much a foreign dialect as that of the Italian." It centered around the idea that Negro speech was full of mispronunciations of words longer than two syllables; a stock laugh in the minstrel shows was the Negro with a lazy tongue who confused a word like "protected" with another of his own invention, like "protecutted." Williams also began to learn stories that could be told while in the blackface character, like the account of his "gran'chilun":

Eddie Cantor

Al Jolson

My gran'chilun is all named after flowers. Dar's Rose and Lillie and de boy, "Artificial," and de las' one was named after parts of de parents' names. De mother named Eliza and de father named Ferdinand, so we call de baby "Federliza."

Dialect jokes illustrating the incorrigible ignorance or sly naivete of the Negro were an essential part of the caricatured role. Bert Williams was to use them for the rest of his stage career.

When Williams felt he had practised enough, he approached music hall employers. With his mild manners and reticence it was weeks before he made a favorable impression, but finally he was offered work at the San Francisco Museum, a music hall where someone was needed to sing in front of the curtain while the sets were being changed backstage. He joined the show, a grueling continuous variety bill, and for his first really professional stint he was offered the sum of $7 a week.

Williams stayed in the San Francisco Museum a few months, leaving in the summer of 1893 to join Martin and Seig's Mastodon Minstrels at another San Francisco theater. The "Mastodon" title was a humorous reference to the fact that the troupe was very small, only five white men and five Negro performers. As the newest member Bert was expected to help shine shoes, press suits, polish the nickel on the banjos, and arrange the ten chairs in a semi-circle on stage before he finally took his place with the troupe each evening. When the theater manager decided to go on a little tour playing to country towns off the railroad lines near San Francisco, he sent Bert downtown to talk to an unemployed minstrel man who the manager thought might join the Mastodon troupe. Williams didn't know it, but the errand marked the first major turning point in his career.

EYES TURNED TOWARD THE EAST

I N THE 1890'S, when vaudeville claimed the spotlight on the American popular stage, it was a rare night's bill that didn't feature a two man team of some sort: comedians, singers, acrobats, or dancers. It was sometimes easier for two newcomers to join forces and appeal to theater managers as a double "attraction" instead of a single unknown. Bert Williams was slowly learning about the theater, and he was willing to try almost anything that would make his act stronger. Walking along Market Street in San Francisco, he stopped to ask a Negro about his own age lounging against a building at the corner of O'Farrell Street where he could locate the actor his manager had suggested. The fellow Bert questioned straightened up, looked back at him confidently, and replied that he didn't know *that* particular actor, but if an end man was needed for a minstrel company, he couldn't recommend anybody in San Francisco who could dance and tell jokes better than he could himself. Bert looked him over carefully and finally replied, "That's good enough. Come on down to rehearsals." Bert Williams had found George Walker, the man who was to be his partner for the next sixteen years.

George Walker was twenty years old when he met Bert, a year older than his new stage partner. Like Williams, he was ambitious and determined to succeed in show business. Born in Lawrence, Kansas, in 1873, the son of a policeman, he had already had years of experience in minstrel and medicine shows. He had a very dark complexion, was several inches shorter than Williams, and was perhaps in some ways more naturally suited than Bert to the minstrel stage. In August, 1906, Walker recalled his boyhood for *Theater Magazine* with what seems to be a characteristic frankness, despite the conventional rewriting of the interviewer.

> The stage has always fascinated me. To stand before the footlights and entertain large audiences has ever been the dream of my life. When but a lad, I joined a company of amateur colored minstrels in my native town, Lawrence, Kansas. There were thirteen of us, but I cannot say that we had bad luck. We gave annual performances, and were always well patronized, and our net receipts from the box were usually gratifying.

A MAGNIFICENT PRODUCTION

OF THAT STERLING HISTORICAL DRAMA

UNCLE TOM'S CABIN

OR LIFE AMONG THE LOWLY.

BY HARRIET BEECHER STOWE.

A HIGH-CLASS ENTERTAINMENT

THE HISTORIC SLAVE MARKET

And many other scenes that go to form a great production of this grand old historical play.

A PAIR OF FULL-BLOODED BLOODHOUNDS

Trained to take part in the Drama, are used in the thrilling scene showing

Eliza Escaping from the Slave-hunters

A GREAT AND MORAL PLAY.

COMING WITH ALL THE GRANDEUR AND MAGNITUDE THAT THE MIND OF MAN EVER CONCEIVED.

BRIGHT NEW SONGS, FUNNY SAYINGS, ORIGINAL JUBILEE SINGERS AND TALENTED MUSICIANS.

A GOOD PERFORMANCE IS ALWAYS WORTHY OF PATRONAGE.

Replete with Comedy and Pathos and mingling with tears in a most marvelous fashion.

SPLENDID SCENERY AND HANDSOME COSTUMES

═ A SUPERB ORCHESTRA ═

A BREATH OF AIR FROM THE SUNNY SOUTH

PLANTATION SONGS AND MELODIES

SEE

The Funny Lawyer, Marks.
The Frolicsome "Topsy."
The Quaint Spinster, Aunt Ophelia.
The Beautiful Little Eva.
The Kind and Affectionate "Uncle Tom"
The Hard-Hearted Legree.
The Abused Mulatto Slave, "Eliza."
The Grand Transformation Scene.

A Play that is Delightful, Wonderful, Instructive and Moral.

LEGREE WHIPPING TOM.

SOME PRACTICAL AND CANDID WORDS

FOR THE MILLIONS OF FATHERS AND MOTHERS
Well Worth Remembering.

If you can afford to visit but one exhibition this season, this is surely the one. As your clergyman will tell you, it will return you both instruction in American history and wholesale recreation more than ten times the price of admission.

It is just what it is advertised to be--the Grandest, Purest and Most Interesting, Instructive and Moral Show on Earth.

THIS SHOW IS DESERVEDLY POPULAR.

It is hard to find a person who has not seen it or doesn't intend to. It is patronized and applauded and endorsed by the clergymen and religious press.

We are accused of but one fault--our visitors exclaim

IT IS DELIGHTFUL, WONDERFUL, INSTRUCTIVE AND MORAL.

DON'T FAIL TO TAKE THE CHILDREN AND GIVE THEM A LASTING LESSON IN AMERICAN HISTORY.

THE PLOT.

I started out with the idea that it was possible for the black performer to do better. My associates shared my views to some extent, but to most of them the future offered little encouragement, and the longer I remained at home the more impossible it seemed for me ever to realize my ambition. So I left Lawrence and went west to California.

There were many quack doctors doing business in the West. They traveled from one town to another in wagons, and gave shows in order to get large crowds of people together, so as to sell medicine. When a boy, I was quite an entertainer. I could sing and dance, and was good at face-making, beating the tamborine and rattling the bones. I was not lacking in courage and did not hesitate to ask the quacks for a job. First one and then the other hired me. When we arrived in a town and our show started, I was generally the first to attract attention. I would mount the wagon and commence to sing and dance, make faces, and tell stories, and rattle the bones. I had to rough it, going across the country this way, and rough it I did. But I got there, and that was the main thing.

When I reached San Francisco, I left the quacks and went around the theaters and music halls looking for employment. While I was hanging around one day, I saw a gaunt fellow over six feet, of orange hue—that was Bert Williams. He was stage struck too! We got a job together at $7 a week each. That was many years ago. We have had ups and downs since those days, but we still hang together.

The "gaunt fellow . . . of orange hue" found himself paired with Walker in the Mastodon Minstrel semi-circle, and they worked up a duet, Bert strumming the banjo while George sang a "coon" song, "See Yer Colored Man." They contrasted effectively on stage, the tall, awkwardly shy West Indian a good foil for the shorter, self-confident boy from Kansas. As a theatrical pair they were like a score of other beginners in San Francisco, but their partnership seemed like a good idea. Bert Williams had struggled futilely for too many months. He was ready to join forces with somebody who might help.

The early years of the Williams and Walker partnership can only be sketchily pieced together, because although they were interviewed many times later when they were successful entertainers, neither Bert nor George cared to talk much about their start in San Francisco. It was as though they agreed that the many unpleasant experiences they encountered before they came to New York were best forgotten. After a brief stint with the Mastodon Minstrels they found work in one of San Francisco's cheapest variety houses, a "free and easy" cabaret called Jack Halahan's Cramorne Theater (its name was later changed to the "Midway Plaisance" after the famous showplace operating at the Chicago World's Fair). The Midway Plaisance was located among beer cellars, cheap restaurants, and dingy theaters in a group of blocks on Market Street known as "The Line." Nearby on the corner was the Cafe Royale billiard parlor, and on the empty lot next to the Cafe, hucksters, freaks, and medicine men performed under canvas tents that were garishly illuminated by flaring torches. Inside the Midway continuous entertainment was offered to customers most of the day and night, with performances from 1:30 P.M. to 4 A.M. Bert and George added their songs and comedy routines to a program of casual vaudeville turns and "blue" skits, and they stayed at the Midway for almost two years, from the winter of 1893 to the fall of 1895.

Try as they might, they were unable to take their act into better theaters. They were booked outside the Midway only once in those years, a short appearance in 1894 at the Mid-Winter Exposition in Golden Gate Park. There the work they were called upon to do added little to their reputation as rising young entertainers, however. The Exposition wasn't much of an enterprise as World Fairs go, relying mostly on a small midway, a ferris wheel, donkey rides, band concerts, stalls selling sponge cake, and a scattering of exhibits, including one of Chiquita, the smallest woman in the world. There were also plans for a model of an African Dahomian village on the fairgrounds, but "when the ship transporting the real savages from Africa was delayed," a call went out to vaudevillians working in San Francisco. Bert and George were among the "natives" hired in the hoax, and for a few weeks they impersonated Dahomians, dressed in animal skins, posing among the potted palm trees.

Back at the Midway Plaisance the partnership featured George Walker as comedian, since his previous years of experience in minstrel shows had given him more facility on stage than Bert had at this time. Williams concentrated on his songs and banjo strumming, acting as straight man for Walker's laughs. They both wore street clothes and didn't use blackface make-up, and in the beginning they were billed as Walker and Williams. After a year at the Midway they flipped a coin to see if their names should remain in the same order on the cardboard sign put out to announce their act. When Bert won the toss, they were thereafter known as "Williams and Walker."

Although they had steady work in San Francisco, the young men were too ambitious to remain there forever. After two years at the Midway it seemed they faced a dead end, since they were unable to break into the major variety circuits. If they wanted a bigger future in the theater they would have to move East. They decided to go to Chicago, where they heard a big Negro show, Isham's *Octoroons,* was performing before large audiences. The most economical way for them to get there was by working their way across country, but the best job they could get at the beginning of winter was performing with a medicine show headed for Texas. In a sense this was a comedown for Walker, who had ridden to California two years before on the back of a similar wagon, but Bert and George were in for a new experience. This trip would be the first time either of them had traveled in the South.

The wagon containing the "doctors," their stock of patent medicines, and Williams and Walker, headed south through the Arizona desert to Texas, the doctors peddling their supplies as they went along. Bert and George did their songs and dances on the small stage at the back of the wagon to audiences who became increasingly less enthusiastic. One afternoon when the wagon had stopped in a small town near El Paso, Bert and George were approached by a small crowd of people who jeered at them and tauntingly questioned them about their clothes, which the country people implied were too good for Negroes. The mob forced them to undress and put on burlap sacking. This incident amused the doctors, but Williams and Walker were furious. Immediately afterwards they left the medicine show and gave up all plans to travel in the Deep South. The hostility they had encountered was no different from the treatment usually given to traveling Negro acts and minstrel companies. In 1897 the young minstrel entertainer Tom Fletcher accepted as an unavoidable professional hazard that "the towns in most of the southern states were very rough to us because the Civil War was still pretty fresh in their minds. . . . townspeople made it very plain that no other colored people were wanted there. Usually they had signs prominently displayed which read, 'Nigger, Read and Run.' And sometimes there would be added 'And if you can't read, run anyhow.' "

Nevertheless, the trouble in Texas with the medicine show made such a deep impression on Williams and Walker that they never, even with their most popular productions, booked themselves into theaters below the Mason-Dixon line. Traveling north as rapidly as possible, they stopped long only at Cripple Creek, Colorado, a boom town fifteen miles west of Colorado Springs, close to Pikes Peak, where they wangled a job at the Topic Theater. They were able to save a little money for the rest of the trip to Chicago, and Bert remembered that they "arrived there with $2 for two and ate up six-bits worth at the first restaurant."

The show they had traveled to Chicago to join, Isham's *Octoroons,* was one of the first Negro companies to attempt entertainment beyond the minstrel programs, an important step in the development of the Negro theater. Many young performers who were later to become outstanding theatrical personalities were given valuable experience with the *Octoroons.* It had been produced in the fall of 1895 in New York by John William Isham, who had been a minstrel show press agent. In the *Octoroons,* performers presented their acts as in a variety theater, without being restricted to the standard minstrel semicircle with formal introductions by the "Interlocutor," but for the most part the entertainment still relied heavily on "coon" songs and humor. As an important added attraction there was a large chorus of young girls who helped to draw the crowds to the box office. Negro women had not had much chance to appear on the stage at that time, since they had not been allowed to become part of the cast in the traditional minstrel shows, which usually had "wench" impersonators. With skillful vaudeville acts and brashly staged finale numbers, the *Octoroons* did very well in New York before beginning extended runs in other cities.

About the time that Williams and Walker arrived in Chicago, John Isham began to rehearse another show, *Oriental America,* scheduled to open in New York in the fall, 1896. When the *Octoroons'* cast began to lose performers rehearsing for the new production, some new acts were needed to keep the old company going. Jesse Shipp, a man about the same age as Williams and Walker, who sang in the show and was Isham's stage manager, auditioned their act and gave them a week's trial engagement with the *Octoroons* at the Pekin Theater. Much to their disappointment, however, Williams and Walker's act left the Chicago audiences cold. They faced a major setback: they were dropped from the *Octoroons'* bill.

Despite their disappointment, their few nights with the successful company showed them what they needed to do to improve their act. As George Walker later explained,

> There were many more barriers in the way of the black performer in those days than there are now, because, with the exception of the Negro minstrels, the black entertainer was little known throughout the Northern and Western states. The opposition on account of racial and color prejudice and the white comedians who "blacked up" stood in the way of the natural black performers.
>
> How to get before the public and prove what ability we might possess was a hard problem for us to solve. We thought that as there seemed to be a great demand for blackfaces on the stage, we would do all we could to get what we felt belonged to us by the laws of nature. We finally decided that as white men with black faces were billing themselves "coons," Williams and Walker would do well to bill themselves as "The Two Real Coons," and so we did. Our bills attracted the attention of managers, and gradually we made our way in.

Despite the ring of sincerity, Walker was not entirely honest in his appraisal of the position of "natural black performers" in 1896. With Williams, he was setting out to exploit one particular facet of Negro music—in the realm of popular entertainment—but there was another aspect of the situation he did not mention. Attempts to present Negro performers with dignity and self-respect had been made as early as the 1870's and 1880's with the tours of the Fisk and Hampton University "Jubilee Singers," student groups who traveled widely in the Northern and Midwestern states. Their concerts of spirituals won such enthusiastic support that they raised over $150,000 during their travels around the country. By the 1890's the Jubilee Singers, as well as several studies of Negro slave songs, had established the value of Negro music to the extent that Anton Dvorak, the composer, then director of the National Conservatory of Music in New York, said, "In the Negro melodies of America I discover all that is needed for a great and noble school of music."

There was a growing tradition of legitimate presentation of Negro material when Williams and Walker chose instead to employ their talents in the "Ethiopian business" of burnt cork caricature. Participating in the comic minstrel show roles based on white actors' burlesque of Negro mannerisms, they assumed stage roles that submerged and degraded any innately personal musical expression. Perhaps realizing this predicament, Williams and Walker attempted to solve the problem by being somewhat special, vaguely conceived of as "the real thing." The closest they could come at first was a new billing. As "The Two Real Coons," they finally landed a job with a small group of entertainers who traveled to towns and summer resorts in the Midwest, putting on variety shows in local theaters and auditoriums. They once more went on the road, trying to make their act more distinctive, and the revisions they made during the spring and summer of 1896 placed them solidly in the category of black-face entertainers.

They began to differentiate their roles more sharply. Walker continued to tell the jokes and act the comedian, but he also emphasized his flair for clothes. He became the dandy, the "Broadway Swell," the standard minstrel show dude characterization. He dressed in flashy street clothes, exaggerated peg top trousers, silk cravats, vests, and two-toned button shoes, with colors and patterns all beyond the standards of careful taste but definitely guaranteed to attract attention. He played the bold and carefree sport who was so self-possessed and triumphant that his posturing verged on the preposterous. In contrast to Walker's flamboyant arrogance, Williams put on his oldest trousers and a mis-matched checked jacket. He had a larger build than Walker, and it seemed natural for Bert to emphasize the awkwardness of his long arms and legs. He shuffled on stage and played straight man to George's clowning before starting to sing his dialect songs.

The contrast in appearance and personalities was a first step, but it took a little longer for them to make their most important discovery—that Bert Williams was a gifted comedian. Ironically, this revelation might not have occurred at all if he had not overcome his natural repugnance and forced himself to black-up one evening in a Detroit theater. Years later, when Williams could recall the incident without rancor, he explained,

> One day at Moore's Wonderland in Detroit, just for a lark, I blacked my face and tried the song, "Oh, I Don't Know, You're Not So Warm." Nobody was more surprised than I was when it went like a house on fire. Then I began to find myself. It was not until I was able to see myself as another person that my sense of humor developed.

Under the burnt cork Bert's natural flair for comic imitations finally found a channel on stage. Reticent and shy by nature, he had lacked a forceful stage personality. Not only was the blackface clown immediately identifiable as a specific comic type, but Bert suddenly discovered he could use it to express his comic ideas. Audiences might have enjoyed the make-up for its familiar associations, but Williams tolerated it only for the opportunity it gave him to gain power as a comedian by being "able to see myself as another person." Naturally reserved, at first he hid behind the blackface make-up; his tragedy was that the mask trapped him, for as the years went by, he could not remove the disguise.

Almost before Williams and Walker had a chance to realize the full possibilities of their new act, they were contacted by a well-known New York theatrical producer, Thomas Canary, who was vacationing at a hotel in French Lick Springs, Indiana, where they were appearing. Canary saw them and was impressed. He promised to put them in a revue he was casting the next winter, but only a short time later Williams and Walker got a telegram from him saying that if they could get to New York by September 14th, they could have an engagement right away in another show, *The Gold Bug*. There was no question about getting to New York in time. They had been in show business long enough to recognize a break when they saw one.

36 CONSECUTIVE WEEKS OF WHAT YOU MAY CALL VELVET

THE *DRAMATIC MIRROR* did more than just mirror stage events in New York City. As the leading theatrical newspaper in the United States, it was not afriad to state its opinions emphatically. It liked some things very much and was unsparingly critical of others. In the 1890's it certainly looked authoritative; its large white sheets were crammed with headlines, long narrow columns of small type, fuzzy photographs of matinee idols, and garishly designed self-congratulatory advertisements. The articles took great pleasure deriding the self-importance of Englishmen like George Bernard Shaw, whose "sublime self-esteem, like the peace of God, passeth understanding." The newspaper also felt that American Negroes should know their place, and words like "coon" and "nigger" were standard components of any review describing a blackface entertainer. The *Dramatic Mirror* enjoyed animal acts, acrobatic tumblers, mechanical lighting effects, and plump chorus girls, and it discussed circuses and traveling tent shows in every issue. It also chronicled the social activities of genteel singers and actors in legitimate plays and operas, when columnists like the "Matinee Girl" reported backstage visits with performers who were the current favorites. Reviewers were quick to expose acts which did not live up to advance publicity: "The Barrison Singers, billed as Parisian dancers, wear French underwear over their pink tights, but the whole five pairs of legs put together would not fill the tights of Edward E. Rice's slimmest chorus girl." Most important for Williams and Walker, however, was the unhappy fact that the *Dramatic Mirror* was not the least impressed by *The Gold Bug*, the show that had brought them to New York.

In the issue of September 26, 1896, the newspaper was brutally specific:

The Gold Bug, a Musical Farce by Glen McDonough and Victor Herbert. Produced September 14 at the Casino Theater. This piece is neither a farce, burlesque or comic opera, but an incongruous blending of all three. The story opens at the Naval Secretary's residence in Washington, where Willet Float, an absconding Indian agent, has in return for enormous campaign contributions, been appointed Secretary of the Navy. Ignorant of naval affairs, Float institutes various reforms which end disastrously. The "Gold Bug" itself is the

29

name of a supposed naval cruiser, aboard which some of the tom-
foolery occurs. The show is pretentious vaudeville, thinly and trans-
parently disguised. The "incidental introductions," as the programme
delicately words it, are merely variety turns. The success of the show
depends on the vaudeville attractions, which are often clever. The
piece is booked to run until November 2.

The next week, on October 3, 1896, the *Dramatic Mirror* curtly reported that "*The Gold Bug* proved to be a very weak insect. After one brief week's existence, it flitted off into obscurity."

The end of the show meant another failure for Victor Herbert, a young man who was to become famous for his operettas in later years, but who had at that time only one small success to his credit, the musical farce *The Wizard of the Nile,* which ran a few months at the Casino Theater in 1895. Like Victor Herbert, Williams and Walker were struggling for a foothold in the theater. They could take a little pride in being part of the variety acts which had received some favorable notice, but they were still out of a job. However, they couldn't feel as worried as they had been in Chicago when they learned that Isham's *Octoroons* didn't want them, for they were surrounded in New York by what looked like vaudevillian paradise. If they had left steady work at the San Francisco Midway to "turn their faces toward the East," they weren't disappointed when they reached Broadway.

Variety was in full swing when Williams and Walker arrived in New York. Scores of theaters, from Oscar Hammerstein's opulent Olympia Roof Garden, decorated with a miniature Italian grotto and a Swiss mountain with real cascades of water, lakes, and an old rustic bridge, to equally famous if less refined Tenderloin dance halls like the Haymarket, were booking hundreds of acts each week. The great majority of the variety turns from the first class to the last class theaters were actually closer to circus life than "high art," with brash acts by entertainers like "The Sport and the Jew" and "The Merry Wops" serving as the mainstay of most programs. Young and relatively inexperienced, Williams and Walker were probably not much better than most of the others, but there was such a demand for talent that they didn't need to have more than a slight edge of assurance. The years they had spent unfailingly turning in some sort of a song and dance routine at the rowdy Midway Plaisance in San Francisco, and their more recent effort to give style to their act during the months in the midwestern summer resorts, stood them in good stead. Besides, they were "coon" performers, and at the turn of the century New York audiences were patronizing many blackface "Tabasco Senegambians."

Lew Dockstader and the team of McIntyre and Heath were the top white men doing blackface acts, and even women like the Paris star Yvette Guilbert had succumbed to the fashion, translating into French several "darky" songs she had bought from the music publishers M. Witmark and Son. Anna Held, another French singer who was being managed by a very young but ambitious man named Florenz Ziegfeld, Jr., sang her songs in English, but they came out sounding like "My Gal Ees a High Bor-r-rn Ladee." Many white American stage beauties like Dainty Kitty Mitchell sang the songs straight, songs that today seem astonishingly cruel and repellant: "He's Just a Little Nigger, but He's

Mine, All Mine"; "Coon, Coon, Coon, How I Wish My Color Would Change"; "Every Race Has A Flag But The Coon"; and "You May Be A Hawaiian On Old Broadway, But You're Just Another Nigger To Me."

Adding to the enthusiasm for "coon" performers, only a few months before Williams and Walker came to New York another entertainment with "a genuine Southern flavor" had become a fad—ragtime. It had been introduced at Tony Pastor's Music Hall in February, 1896, by Ben Harney, a twenty-five year old song writer from Kentucky. Within a few days, the catchy syncopation of his piano pieces and tap dances were imitated all over town. White entertainers who sang or played "con expressione with much de color" were available in great quantities in New York, but there was still a demand for performers who were willing to take on the caricature role. Williams and Walker didn't have to wait long for a job. They had held their own with the other specialty acts in *The Gold Bug,* and a few days after it closed they were included with several other "incidental performers" from the show into the cast of the Peter Dailey Company, a stock company that had a two week booking in Boston. The prospect of leaving New York within a month of their first arrival was disheartening, but Williams and Walker were too poor to refuse a job. Without knowing it, they were right on the verge of what Walker later remembered as "36 consecutive weeks of what you may call velvet."

After Boston, when the Peter Dailey Company returned to New York, Williams and Walker got their biggest break. George Lederer, who had been one of the producers of *The Gold Bug,* introduced them to William A. McConnell, the man who booked acts at the popular Koster and Bial's Music Hall, at 34th Street and Broadway. Business was so good that as a personal favor to his friend Lederer, McConnell agreed to let them have a week's trial engagement. The music hall was attracting crowds of spectators nightly because it was showing a "Wonderfully real and singularly exhilarating" novelty, the moving picture, that had made its debut at Koster and Bial's on April 23, 1896. The *Dramatic Mirror* was duly informed of McConnell's decision; it announced in its October 31, 1896 issue that "the new attraction this week at Koster and Bial's will be Williams and Walker, colored performers who are coming rapidly to the front." In its next issue, the newspaper covered their opening night, helping to spread the word about the new act at the music hall.

> *Williams and Walker made their first Eastern appearance in high class vaudeville here and scored an immediate success. The dude member of the team does various funny walks, and the common every-day Nigger has only to open his mouth to bring laughs. He has a deep voice and sings a song called "Oh, I Don't Know, You Ain't So Wahm," with the greatest possible unction. The song would not be much use to anyone but him, and he makes the most of it. Their act is rather crude, and if it were properly fixed by an expert farce writer, it would be an immense hit.*

Williams and Walker found a receptive audience on Broadway. Trying to give the public what it wanted, they settled further into their roles. Bert was getting the most applause with his song, "Oh, I Don't Know, You Ain't So Wahm," but they needed something to follow this number and conclude their act. In the last week of November they introduced "two coffee-colored ladies dressed in yellow" for a grand cakewalk finale. This did the trick. The *Dramatic Mirror* announced on January 23, 1897, that Williams and Walker had been given an indefinite run at Koster and Bial's.

What was the act that was going over so well? It was essentially the same partnership that had failed in Chicago (Jesse Shipp, who had been with Isham's *Octoroons,* met them later in New York and said, "When I saw what a hit the boys had made, I was very much surprised; not that I didn't think they both had ability, because I knew they had, but with us they had not even pleased"), but with one important difference: Williams was playing the role of comedian.

When he had blacked up for the first time at Moore's Wonderland in Detroit, Williams had found a way to express his innate gifts for comedy. Walker let him take over more of the laugh lines, and they differentiated their characterizations so that there was more interplay between Williams, the awkward, stubbornly bumbling clown, and Walker, the arrogant, flamboyant dandy. They were in blackface projecting the "coon" stereotypes for all they were worth, really indistinguishable from a score of other variety blackface acts; except that Bert, from the beginning, communicated a special "unction" that audiences found particularly appealing. He had accepted the degrading make-up, but behind it he was slowly shaping a unique comic personality.

The reputation of "The Two Real Coons" grew steadily. In March, 1897, they were still at Koster and Bial's and the *Dramatic Mirror* reported, "They have made a hit which has placed them in the front rank of the top liners." Within six months of their arrival in New York, Williams and Walker were described as two of the leading Negro stars in vaudeville. Koster and Bial's had suggested they go under the management of William A. McConnell, and encouraged by their quick New York success, McConnell even booked them abroad, into the Empire Music Hall in London for a week in April, where they were only mildly received.

But back in New York throughout the summer of 1897 they were "the celebrated delineators of darky characters." They left to clown on the Keith circuit in Boston, then returned to New York to play Hammerstein's Olympia Roof Garden and Tony Pastor's Music Hall, appearing in every first class variety house in the city. Everywhere they went, they were "the hit of the bill." By the end of the summer they had played almost all the major houses in Boston and New York. For the new fall season they could repeat their acts, but it seemed wiser to try something new. Their manager William McConnell advised them to strengthen their reputation by joining a good vaudeville troupe and touring the country, so they signed with the Hydes' Comedians company, a show which starred the blackface comedy team McIntyre and Heath, as well as the acts of several other variety headliners: singers, acrobats, a trained dog and monkey act, and a comic burglar musician. McIntyre and Heath had been popular for twenty years and were to continue for yet another twenty years relying on the same blackface parody, "The Georgia Minstrels," a combination of anecdotes and funny repartee that emphasized the stumbling mistakes of Heath and the pompous portly figure of McIntyre. Williams and Walker were in the company of very proficient professionals when they joined Hydes' Comedians, but they easily held their own.

From October, 1897, to May, 1898, Bert and George traveled with Hydes' Comedians, finishing the season in San Francisco at the Orpheum Theater, a much classier theater than the Midway Plaisance on Market Street. They had done well with the Comedians, although they might have felt a little self-conscious playing on the same bill with McIntrye and Heath's expert blackface parody. Nevertheless, Williams and Walker had become such skillful imitators of the white man's conception of the Negro that their performances didn't seem out of place. Their stage personalities had become sufficiently adjusted to what audiences expected.

One season playing second-fiddle to other blackface delineators was enough. When Williams and Walker got back to New York they saw McDonnell again. He agreed that they couldn't advance much further with Hydes' Comedians, and that it would be better if they could be placed in a production that featured them more prominently. Unfortunately he didn't know of any such show—at the present time. Booked into Koster and Bial's Williams and Walker returned to the music hall circuit the summer of 1898, dancing and singing as the celebrated cakewalkers. They were continually winning praise as the best in the business, but what they could do with the prize cake was still undetermined.

33

THE GENUINE EXPLOITATION OF THE NOW FAMOUS CAKEWALK

ADA PATTERSON, a reporter for a New York magazine featuring a series of reprints of the most popular songs of the day, called on Bert Williams in the summer of 1898, and later she wrote about the meeting.

I rapped on a worn sagging door. A brief delay and the door opened. In the doorway as a portrait in a frame, stood a tall dark figure, exceedingly tall. His neatly tailored black suit lent him a special sombreness. The features were calm as those of a bronze—a weather-beaten bronze in Central Park. The eyes were large, but quiet and sad.

Yes, he was Mr. Williams. Yes, he would be glad to have one of the Williams and Walker songs published. It would be necessary for me to see the composer, Will Marion Cook.

He apologized for the darkness of the stairway and its five flights. He warned me to "take them slow and easy."

In 1898 Bert Williams may have been a headliner at the most fashionable vaudeville theaters in town, but he and Walker lived on the top floor of a cheap apartment on Fifty-third Street. Although they were earning good salaries, they felt the years of financial scrambling before their New York triumph still close behind them. They were both young, in their early twenties, and unaccustomed to living extravagantly. George's first thought was to enlarge his wardrobe. He began to patronize a custom tailor and discarded his "ready mades." He greatly preferred that his suits, shirts, and cravats were the only ones of their kind, and he began to get a reputation as a dandy both on and off the stage. Williams was much less flamboyant. Unlike his partner, who seemed to expand under the pressures of advancing in show business, Bert kept to himself. He showed his tension by drinking more heavily and beginning to chain smoke, a habit he continued for years. Disinterested in living ostentatiously, Williams sent money home to his parents in Riverside, California, and continued to wear his plain black suits. But one afternoon he stopped at a jewelry store and celebrated his New York success by buying himself a three-stone diamond ring. It was the only costly piece of jewelry he ever wore.

The shabby apartment house on Fifty-third Street became a meeting place where vaudevillians like Harry Burleigh, Will Accoo, Cole and Johnson, and Jesse Shipp could sit around in their shirtsleeves and talk, drink, and play endless hands of a poker game called "smut." Bert once explained it: "We had a sooty plate that we smoked up over the lamp, and the loser of each hand had to smear a daub of the soot on his face as a penalty. Then we kids would sit around and howl at the grotesque appearance."

Highly ambitious, the young men were eager to go as far as possible in show business. George Walker found that "By having these men around us, we had the opportunity to study the musical and theatrical ability of the most talented members of our race." The latest craze was the cakewalk, and all of them were involved in the dance.

In the 1890's the cakewalk was as popular as the Charleston, the jitter-bug, and the twist were to be in later years. The origins of the dance itself are uncertain, but it probably began on the slave plantations. Since the high-kicking, prancing walk-around fitted naturally into the rambunctious minstrel shows, "peregrinating for the pastry" often became the grand finale parade by the entire cast. In 1877 Harrigan and Hart included the feature "Walking for dat Cake, an Exquisite Picture of Negro Life and Customs," among the acts in their New York theater. But the cakewalk craze didn't catch fire until several years later, when suddenly throughout the country appeared a rush of cakewalk contests and extravaganzas. In 1892 the First Annual Cakewalk Jubilee was instituted at Madison Square Garden, a three night contest that featured variety acts as well as a national cakewalk competition for dancers who had won small town contests. The following year, Negro vaudevillians Charlie Johnson and Dora Dean brought a new style and grace to the dance in Sam T. Jack's touring company, the *Creole Show*. They were so universally admired that the *Dramatic Mirror* lowered its ban against printing Negro photographs that were not paid advertisements and ran their picture over the heading "Popular Colored Artists." Johnson and Dean used a gimmick, the "flicker kinetoscope," to enhance their dancing. Wearing dark formal clothes and white gloves, they would give the impression on the stage of the whirl of a hundred hands and feet in the blur of the special spotlight. Williams and Walker were so impressed by Dora Dean's beauty that they wrote a song about her, with the chorus

> *Say, have you ever seen Miss Dora Dean,*
> *She is the finest gal you've ever seen,*
> *I'm a-goin' try and make this gal my queen*
> *Next Sunday mornin' I'm goin' to marry Miss Dora Dean.*

Other cakewalk acts, elaborate skits like Billie and Willie Farrell's "Cakewalk Wedding," using different steps and poses to show the athletic couple's flirtation, meeting, courtship, engagement, wedding, and honeymoon, kept the dance popular in vaudeville. Isham's *Octoroons* show had a cakewalk finale in 1895-6, and in June, 1897, the Black Patti Company advertised its cake was

35

made by the most prominent caterer in New York. A funny finish to the walk is brought about by the entrance of a bad man who wants to know why he was not invited. Razors and pistols are produced and the walk ends in great confusion.

The "bad man" finish was a forecast of an actual event at the Annual Madison Square Garden competition in September, 1897, when angry Negro contestants took the manager, John H. Jenkins, to the nearby police station and argued unsuccessfully that racial prejudice had influenced the awards.

Williams and Walker are so strongly identified with the dance that theater history has traditionally appointed them its originators, but when they first came to New York they were only two of the many blackface song and dance men who were using the cakewalk as part of their act. The distinctiveness of their routine was the combination of George's agility and finesse and Bert's clumsy shoulder-shrugging ineptitude. Bert's humorous efforts were especially incongruous set against the skill of the other dancers. Besides being a master of eccentric steps, George rehearsed the small company of fourteen dancers until their act at Koster and Bial's was unusually smooth and lively. First he and Bert came on together and sang "coon" songs, then they left the stage to be followed by a drum major, jiggling a baton. He led in a master of ceremonies, in dress suit and heavy blackface, who introduced each of the seven fancifully dressed couples who competed for the cake. When Williams and Walker finally came back with two pretty girls with "the cafe au lait complexions," everything was set for them to win the cake with their ludicrous burlesque of the others' eccentric steps.

After watching the "colored fun" in clubs like Koster and Bial's, wealthy New Yorkers tried to cakewalk, often with humorous support from the Negro professional dancers. As a publicity stunt Williams and Walker even called at the Vandervilt mansion and respectfully left a letter with the butler:

To Mr. William K. Vanderbilt
Corner of Fifty-second Street and Fifth Avenue
New York

Dear Sir:

In view of the fact that you have made a success as a cake-walker, having appeared in a semipublic exhibition and having posed as an expert in that capacity, we, the undersigned world-renowned cake-walkers, believing that the attention of the public has been distracted from us on account of the tremendous hit which you have made, hereby challenge you to compete with us in a cake-walking match, which will decide which of us shall deserve the title of champion cake-walker of the world. . . .

Yours very truly,

WILLIAMS AND WALKER

The last paragraph of the letter offered a $50 reward in addition to the World

Champion title. Commenting on the incident later, Bert is supposed to have said, "It was a shame to take his money."

The cakewalk did more than establish Williams and Walker as dancing masters for the cafe society set; it also brought George Walker his wife. In the summer of 1898, when Williams and Walker had returned from their western tour with Hydes' Comedians, a prominent cigaret manufacturer asked them to pose for an advertisement, presumably to show that smoking his brand of cigarets was as much fun as dancing the cakewalk. Stella Wiley, who had been one of the dancers in their Koster and Bial's act, was available for the photograph, but Walker needed another girl to complete the quartet. Stella brought a friend with her, Ada Overton, a very pretty young dancer who lived in Harlem with her mother, and the advertising photograph was taken.

The cigaret manufacturer found the picture so popular with his clients that he asked for another pose. Impressed with the new dancer, Walker began to ride up to Harlem, trying to get her to join his act, but the girl's mother, who didn't want her daughter on the stage, refused to let her consider his offer. The generous financial terms of the second advertisement changed her mind, and Ada Overton was allowed to cakewalk.

Ada soon became as popular as her partner. She had a beautiful figure and, like Walker, wore clothes with a great deal of style. Very ambitious and talented, she developed into an actress of considerable ability when she later played the important feminine roles in the Williams and Walker company. Ada (whose name was sometimes spelled Aida) was born in New York in 1880, and by the time she was sixteen she was an accomplished dancer. She tried to persuade her mother to let her go on the stage, but only after months of argument was she allowed to join the most respectable Negro show, run by the concert singer Madame Sissieretta Jones, also called the Black Patti. Each year the Black Patti Company traveled throughout the United States playing in hundreds of towns and cities, and after a season with the show Ada returned home so exhausted that her mother refused to let her continue on the stage. But the following year, after George Walker assured Ada's mother that she would be dancing in only the best New York theaters, Ada resumed her career.

She was kept busy with the Williams and Walker company. Not only did she star in the cakewalk exhibitions in the music halls, but she also attended after-theater parties at Delmonico's Restaurant, where George brought her to help teach wealthy gentlemen—and their wives—the finer touches of the dance. Before very long, George Walker found himself in love.

By the end of the summer, 1898, Williams and Walker's months of cake-walking finally paid off. They were given the opportunity of appearing in an operetta, *Clorindy, or The Origin of the Cake Walk. Clorindy* had been written by Will Marion Cook and Scott Dunbar, two young men who had been frequent visitors at the Fifty-third Street apartment. Cook, a wide-eyed, light skinned man with a flowing mustache, had recently returned from Europe, where he had studied with Dvorak. Cook was a lively, gregarious man, and once back in New York he became interested in popular Negro music. Dunbar, the poet, had a brooding dark face and was much more shy. His first book, *Lyrics of*

Lowly Life, had been praised highly by the *New York Times,* which called Dunbar "a true singer of the people." A week before the premier of *The Gold Bug,* the show that brought Williams and Walker to New York, Dunbar had given a poetry reading "before an invited audience" at the Lyceum Theater. The *Dramatic Mirror* had been more enthusiastic about his reading than it had been about the musical, although the highest compliment the newspaper could manage was a condescending comparison of his talent to that of James Whitcome Riley's.

> *Paul Dunbar proved a charming entertainer, with a rich, clear voice, an easy manner and a magnetic presence. His gift of versifying is as good as James Whitcome Riley's. Verses in the dialect of his race are of the highest order of excellence, showing the poet's intuitive appreciation of the humor, pathos, and music of lowly life, plus his felicitous gift of versifying.*

By training and inclination, both Cook and Dunbar were primarily interested in serious music and poetry, but after meeting Negro vaudevillians in New York, they were persuaded to collaborate on a short operetta in the spring of 1898, Dunbar writing the lyrics to Cook's songs. *Clorindy* was widely heralded as a feature summer attraction at the Casino Roof Garden, and the lead role was given to a Negro comedian named Ernest Hogan, who advertised himself as "The Creative Comedian and Great Unbleached American" in the pages of the *Dramatic Mirror.* Hogan had starred with the Black Patti Company, and like Williams and Walker, was looking for a leading role with his own show. *Clorindy* seemed to be it.

Dunbar and Cook had had little contact with the popular stage before starting to write their musical. They had been aroused by the ambition of men like Williams and Walker, whose conversation had convinced the young poet and composer that one of the main obstacles for the Negro in overcoming racial stereotypes was a lack of original, creative material. Trying to come up with fresh ideas, Dunbar and Cook planned an operetta that called for an all-Negro cast. With commercial success in mind they decided to woo the crowds to the box office by promising a show that described "the origins of the cakewalk." Their idea was so attractive that Ernest Hogan soon agreed to star in their operetta, and since he had sufficient box office appeal, the manager of the Casino Roof Garden booked the show for the summer.

Because of Will Cook's inexperience (he was fond of tearing up the score when he didn't approve of the way the cast was performing) *Clorindy* wasn't ready until late July, 1898. When it finally opened audiences found an hour-long musical show that was closer to a variety bill than an operetta. With a cast of forty Negro singers and dancers, and a twenty minute cakewalk finale, the Southern plantation love story featuring dusky belles and cotton bales was innocuous summer entertainment. Hogan's songs, "Jump Back Honey," "Who Dat Say Chicken in Dis Crowd," "Hottest Coon in Dixie," and "Darktown Is Out Tonight," were of the standard "coon" variety, despite their being by Cook and Dunbar. With all the good intentions of writing more substantial material for their friends, Cook and Dunbar had just added another blackface vaudeville revue to the repertoire.

THE BIG FEATURE OF E.E.RICE'S "SUMMER NIGHT'S".

WHO DAT SAY CHICKEN IN DIS CROWD.

THE GREAT SUCCESS OF
"CLORINDY"
OR
"THE ORIGIN OF THE CAKE-WALK"

WORDS BY
PAUL LAURENCE DUNBAR.

MUSIC BY
WILL MARION.
5

PUBLISHED BY
M. WITMARK & SONS.
NEW YORK   CHICAGO.
CHAS. SHEARD & CO. LONDON ENG. — WHALEY ROYCE & CO. TORONTO, CAN.
COPYRIGHTED FOR GREAT BRITAIN & ALL BRITISH COLONIES & POSSESSIONS.
SUCCESS IS WORK

Williams and Walker were invited to take over Hogan's role in September, when Hogan decided to return for another season with the Black Patti Company. *Clorindy* had drawn just about all the audience it could in New York, so McConnell booked it into theaters in Boston, Philadelphia, Cincinnati, and Washington, D.C. Twenty more dancers were also added to the company to push "the genuine exploitation of the now famous cakewalk."

Two years after their first arrival in New York, Williams and Walker headed a company of sixty performers, including Will Marion Cook conducting a small "ragtime" orchestra. With a month's assured booking in theaters in major Eastern cities, they had progressed faster than they had ever dreamed possible, but they soon found that their extraordinary success was only temporary. *Clorindy* wasn't a strong enough operetta around which to organize the large cast, even with the featured talents of Ed Goggin and Charles Davis, acrobats, or Black Carl, the magician. When the Senegambian Carnival didn't attract large crowds, the expenses of the company proved greater than their intake at the box office, and the show was disbanded. Williams and Walker were again looking for work. They returned to vaudeville in New York City with a booking at Proctor's Theater, but they were reduced to a company of fifteen, doing a forty minute cakewalk sketch. They were back to where they had been before they joined Hydes' Comedians.

Discouraged, they tried to improve matters by switching their management to the office of Hurtig and Seamon, who offered to form a new Williams and Walker company. There was an important difference in the two managers: previously McConnell had gotten them into good theaters, with high admission prices and a more discriminating clientele. Hurtig and Seamon placed their shows in cheaper theaters, but they proposed that bigger crowds would make a Williams and Walker company a financial success. In one sense they were taking a step down in accepting Hurtig and Seamon's proposal, but Walker was willing to gamble if it meant getting the large company he wanted. Williams went along with the deal; he trusted his partner's judgment.

The gamble worked. In January, 1899, a new arrangement of the old "Senegambian" standards, now advertised as *A Lucky Coon,* began to play one night stands in Hartford, New Haven, New London, Meridan, Waterbury, Providence, Brooklyn, Harlem, and Philadelphia. It was "a hodge-podge of nearly everything in the coon line, from buck-dancing and ragtime melodies to selections from grand opera," but new audiences found it "capital entertainment." In February the company moved into the midwest, touring Dayton, Chicago, Milwaukee, and St. Louis; then East to Cleveland, Buffalo, and Washington. Everywhere they went, they cakewalked, from the smallest theater in Waterbury to the "grand carnival jubilee" in the First Regimental Armory in Chicago. The polished cakewalk act that had entertained the New York social register was appearing before less sophisticated—but enthusiastic—audiences, and Williams and Walker and their "latest ebony specialties" seemed set. Under the management of Hurtig and Seamon, *A Lucky Coon* was suddenly as successful as any of the other raffish Negro companies touring the nation.

THE BUD IF NOT THE FLOWER

A T THE END of the nineteenth century, Americans were entertained by extravagance. They liked a conglomeration of strong details, turrets and gingerbread cornices on their houses; ostrich feather boas, frilly laces, and stiff bustles on their women. Even games became a production—people wore what would now be considered formal attire to hit croquet balls or swing away at shuttlecock. Since their everyday lives were tightly ordered by earnest industry and limited leisure, they came to the theater for sprawling visions, for Roman spectacles rather than Sabbath simplicity. Ten years before, in the 1880's, a show like *Uncle Tom's Cabin* could entertain audiences with a small company of actors who doubled the parts and displayed further accomplishment in the "olio" or vaudeville acts which followed the play. As Tom Fletcher said, "In the early period . . . you were not hired or even considered in show business unless you could sing, dance, talk, tumble, and play some instrument in a brass band." But when Williams and Walker came before the public in *A Lucky Coon,* times had changed. The audiences demanded bigger shows, more specialty acts, exciting parades like the extravaganza advertised by Salter and Martin's *Uncle Tom* show in 1896:

THE GREATEST THING THAT EVER HAPPENED!

A special novelty, Entirely New, the Pride of Louisiana, Mlle. Malvina Moreau's Creole Ladies' Band, the Only One in Existence, Male and Female Pickaninny Singers and Dancers, the Nashville Students Quartet, the Famous Georgia Shouters, Champion Buck and Wing Dancers, Three Bands (Whose Members Do Not Double on the Stage): Creole Ladies' Band, White Band of Sixteen Prominent Solo Artists, Pickaninny Band of Fourteen Southern Darky Boys, Also Twelve Siberian Bloodhounds and Three Shetland Ponies; Own Calcium Effects and Electrical Apparatus!

The companies might advertise themselves as "The Greatest Thing That Ever Happened," but they were for the most part a string of thinly disguised vaudeville turns supporting the perennial "uncle Tom" plot. The music depended heavily on sentimental ballads and dialect comedy songs; the characterizations were loosely modeled on the old racial stereotypes. Although Negro songs and dances had had considerable influence on American popular entertainment in the 1830's and 1840's, serving as the impetus for the development of the white man's minstrel show, the situation had changed by the end of the century, when Negro entertainers themselves were finally allowed a fuller participation in show business. In the fifty years of minstrelsy, the "Ethiopian" showmen, both white and Negro, had wandered far from any fresh or original statement. The shows became bigger, but the material had nearly run dry. It seemed that colored performers were stuck in the conventions of die-hard minstrel patterns, although at this time more vital forms of musical expression were developing among Negroes themselves in the rural blues and city jazz styles. These were not to emerge and influence American popular entertainment for another twenty years, however, until after World War I.

Far from their folk roots, "coon" songs and shows were without much distinction in the 1890's. They amused audiences with annual novelties, but as entertainment they had a place far down in the theatrical ladder. The touring Negro shows—Williams and Walker's *A Lucky Coon,* the Black Patti Troubadours, Cole and Johnson's *A Trip to Coontown,* John Isham's *Octoroons, Oriental America, Darkest America, Black America, The South Before the War*— were considered far beneath "legitimate" plays which toured with top stars to play the first rate theaters; events like Henry Miller touring in *The Only Way,* or E. H. Sothern in *The King's Musketeers,* or Mrs. Leslie Carter ("The American Bernhardt") in *Zaza.* Operas and symphony concerts usually also played first or second rate theaters, as did Shakespearian revivals, plays like *Nathan Hale* and *The Second Mrs. Tanquary,* or even melodramas like *Quo Vadis,* all touring at the end of the century. Less "legitimate" generally were the vaudeville bills, but here as in the drama there was a hierarchy of stars and companies. Chancey Olcott or Weber and Fields played better theaters than those billing undistinguished performers like Kelley and Mason in their farce *Maloney's Wedding.* Under Hurtig and Seamon's booking office, Williams and Walker—like the other Negro companies—were in the lowest bracket.

If their show was artistically a little above the level of the other Negro productions, it was a credit to George's indefatigable management, since the bulk of the vaudevillians in the Williams and Walker troupe had been recruited from the touring shows or summer tent extravaganzas.

Although there were many Negro actors, singers, dancers, and musicians in the United States in 1899, Bert and George considered only three of them— the Black Patti, Ernest Hogan, and Bob Cole—major competitors. These personalities also headed companies touring the second and third rate theaters, struggling to put together some sort of novelty each year to entice fresh audiences, sometimes only just barely maintaining themselves in the face of competition from circuses or revival meetings. With *A Lucky Coon,* Williams and Walker assumed a place next to the other big Negro stars in their league.

The entertainment business flourished so luxuriantly in the last years of the nineteenth century that it frequently permitted doubles. There was, for example, the magnificent Nellie Melba, who inspired a Negro singer, Madame Flowers, to call herself the "Bronze Melba," qualifying for the title on the basis of a voice which some critics insisted could be heard on Tenth Avenue when she sang in Madison Square Garden. The Italian operatic soprano, Adelina Patti, found great adulation and wealth from her loyal following in America, and her Negro namesake, otherwise known as Madame M. Sissieretta Jones, alias the Black Patti, held her own before different, but also appreciative, crowds.

Madame Jones, who headed the Black Patti Troubadours for nineteen years, from its first season in 1896 to its last in 1915, was born Matilda S. Joyner in Portsmouth, Virginia, in 1868. Her family moved north to Rhode Island when she was four years old, and when she showed musical talent, she took voice lessons at the New England Conservatory in Boston. She began to appear on concert programs in 1887, and the following year she sang at Wallack's Theater, which was, as press releases informed the public, "a place where no other colored singer had been privileged to shine." Under skillful management, she left the United States to add luster to her reputation by touring the West Indies and South America, and in 1891 she was back concertizing in the United States, a featured artist in the 1892 Cakewalk Jubilee at Madison Square Garden. It was at this time that New York *Clipper* dubbed her "The Black Patti," perhaps partly inspired by the fact that "Whenever she appears in public her breast is seen brilliantly illuminated with some of the most chaste medals extant."

Miss Matilda Joyner became Madame Jones by a marriage to Dick Jones, a one-eyed impresario who had definite plans for his talented wife. He changed her name to M. Sissieretta Jones, then eagerly fastened on the *Clipper's* title, "The Black Patti." But because his wife was very dark skinned, with Negroid features, he took her to London in 1890 to begin the arsenic "treatment," which was supposed to lighten her coloring and straighten her hair. By 1896, Madame Jones had gone as far as her husband thought it was possible for her to go with concerts and private salon "musicales," and he planned a new area of exploitation. The Black Patti formed a musical touring company of her own.

The new company was modeled on the *Oriental America* show, which in 1896 was the first Negro production (although owned and managed by a white man, John Isham) to play on Broadway. Dick Jones wasn't crusading for the cause of serious music. He wanted box office appeal, so around the "magnificent voice, pleasing personality and fine figure" of his wife, he cast the paraphernalia of the "coon" show.

Mme. M. Sissieretta Jones' impressive reputation was the first recommendation for the Black Patti's Fifty Troubadours, but crowds were further enticed by the promise of "Three Hours of Mirth and Melody," beginning with a "Merry Musical Skit entitled 'At Jolly Coon-ey Island.'" The evening's program, widely publicized in "flyers," advance notices circulated in the towns before the show arrived, gave full account of the entertainment. Besides the musical skit, the Troubadours presented a vaudeville olio, with vocal duets, comedians, dancers, and comedy acrobats. The finale was an "Operatic Kaleidoscope," the Black Patti and "forty trained Voices" singing such popular numbers as "Silent Heroes" from *The Chimes of Normandy,* "The Anvil Chorus" from *Il Trovatore,* and a "Medley of National Airs."

Within a year, the show advertised itself as "America's Premier Rag-time Entertainers, the Big Novelty, the Phenomenal Success, the Standard of Merit." Unsophisticated Americans enjoyed the blackface contortionists in the farce that opened the program, and left the theater pleasantly gratified by their own ability to appreciate "serious" operatic singing. The hodge-podge appealed to such a wide range of tastes—all of them unrefined—that the Troubadours traveled thousands of miles each year, playing a grueling forty-five week season from July to May, spending a night in every city and town that had an available theater or a large meeting hall. By 1899, the *Dramatic Mirror* announced that "The Black Patti is without doubt the greatest singer of the race before the public," and in their Christmas issue, 1899, the newspaper listed her company among the top theatrical attractions of the season. The same issue even carried an ad which showed she was famous enough to be parodied.

GEORGE G. GILLIGAN!

A New Monologue Artist, the Novelty Monologue entitled THE BLACKER PATTI. This is a black face act, but my—how different—nothing conventional about it—it's novel and they scream.

BOOK ME QUICK!

Whatever Madame Jones thought of Gilligan's travesty, she insisted on an impeccable aura of pretentious respectability about her. Her favorite photograph showed her wearing a long, heavily embroidered gown with an elaborate train, standing with her back to the camera, her face in profile, her right hand on a white Grecian pedestal. In her private life, she tried to be discreet; in 1900, after separating from Dick Jones, she "married" Rudolph Voelckel, a Jewish business man who took over the management of the company. They traveled together for fifteen years in what was advertised as a $30,000 private railroad car fitted with gold plush upholstery and hand-carved pianos. Eubie Blake, the Negro showman who joined the troupe as a youngster, serving as Madame Jones' private errand boy with regular orders to run to grocery stores for a nickel's worth of her favorite ginger snaps, remembered that Voelckel insisted that a red carpet had to be laid on the sidewalk from the stage door to the hack every time she came to and from the theater.

In the nineteen seasons that the Black Patti Troubadours toured the country, their shows remained basically the same, only changing the personnel as performers came, gained experience, then left the company. The Black Patti never tried anything more ambitious than the novelty of a new hour-long farce every few years. "The Spanish Review," after the Spanish-American War, was a favorite number; "Jolly Coon-ey Island" was revived for many seasons. Unwilling to keep up with the new Negro shows that offered more elaborate revues or operettas, the Troubadours attracted smaller and smaller houses, finally only playing before the least critical audiences. Although the Black Patti claimed the highest respectability in her advertisements, her shows actually had the unfortunate effect of displaying and fostering the ugly racial caricatures in every hamlet in the country. Moreover, while skits like "Jolly Coon-ey Island" furnished experience for hundreds of young Negro entertainers, they also sanctioned the continuance of the burlesqued blackface character into the next generation. It was years before an artist like Marian Anderson avoided the mistakes of the Black Patti and attempted a more serious musical career.

I DON'T LIKE NO CHEAP MAN!

Arr. by W. H. Tyers.

Words & Music by Williams & Walker.

Andante moderato.

mf

Slower till Voice.

p

1. Miss
2. Miss
3. Last

p

Simp-son had al-ways been considered de fin-est gal in town, She
Simp-son was kind o' par-tial to ice-cream and lemon-ade, So
week, at a festi-val, she met Sam Long, folks said he had lots of dough! "Can

p

was de en-vy of all de men dat lived for miles a-round. Last
when Ephraim ask'd her to have some, "Wid pleasure, sir!" she said. She
I 'scort you down to de table," said he,"'Twould be a plea-sure, sho!" At de

week,Bill Johnson took her out to see de minstrels at de hall, He
ate two dish-es of the cream,she says to him, "Ain't you gwine to hab none?" He
ta-ble,Sam grabb'd up the bill o'fare,she said,"I'll take a piece o' chicken wid you!" He

bought de seats in de gal-le-ry, and she didn't like that at all.
says,"I'm waiting for to see if I can stand the blow, if I kin, den I'll hab some."
said, "I am sorry, but I'm 'shy' to-night, won't a nice ham sandwich do?"

Piu Allegro.

She said, "I don't like no cheap man Dat spends his mon-ey on de

p

585—3

'stalment plan; Dat's de rea-son I al-ways car-ry with me 'Nuf

money for what I want. I got a sweet dis-po-sition as any - - one, But

'sakes a - live', I hate to be done, In front of de people dat's

sitting here, too. You's a cheap man, and you won't do!" She said do!".....

Ernest Hogan and Bob Cole, the other two Negro personalities who had something of the Williams and Walker mixture of ambition and talent, were both alumni of the Black Patti show. Ernest Hogan especially tried all his life to give an air of dignity to his career, bragging that his "Chicago friends predict I will make a place in the drama as Laurence Dunbar has in literature." Unfortunately his bravado only thinly covered a fundamental instability that limited his achievement in the theater.

Ernest Hogan, whose real name was Reuben Crowders, was born in Bowling Green, Kentucky, shortly after the Civil War. He left home as a young boy to travel with "Uncle Tom" shows and summer tent companies, singing and dancing, trying to write his own songs. Not much is known about his early years and Hogan remained one of the scores of anonymous Negro entertainers until the late 1890's, when he "composed" one of the most popular—and offensive—numbers in the "coon" song genre, "All Coons Look Alike To Me." As Hogan later described the background of the syncopated ragtime tune, he first heard it in Chicago when he was seeking "a little sport" in the red light district around Pogue and Taylor Streets. Wandering into a saloon, Hogan found a piano player who seemed to have something on his mind. The pianist

was plunking and talking to himself. The tune sounded good, but I could not hear the words, so I went over to the piano and offered him a drink and asked him to play the tune over again. I stayed in Chicago a few weeks and the tune and words haunted me. Each night found me in that same house asking him to play and sing that song.

It seemed that his girl friend had put him out the day I first went there, telling him that "all pimps look alike to me." There was no protection for songs in those days, so when I left Chicago the song left with me. I changed his words and music in the verse but kept the same music in the chorus. . . . We Negroes have been called every name under the sun, so I added another. The coon is a very smart animal, so I gave the song the title "All Coons Look Alike To Me."

> *Talk about a coon having trouble,*
> *I think I have enough of ma own,*
> *It's all about ma Lucy Janey Stubbles,*
> *And she has caused my heart to mourn.*
> *Thar's another coon barber from Virginia,*
> *In soci'ty he's the leader of the day,*
> *And now ma honey gal is gwine to quit me,*
> *Yes, she's gone and drove this coon away.*
> *She'd no excuse, to turn me loose,*
> *I've been abused, I'm all confused,*
> *'Cause these words she did say:*
>
> *(Chorus)*
> *All coons look alike to me.*
> *I've got another beau, you see,*
> *And he's just as good to me as you, nig!*

Ever tried to be.
He spends his money free,
I know we can't agree,
So I don't like you now how,
All coons look alike to me.

Hogan hadn't thought up the name "coon" because it was "a very smart animal"; the name had been used for years as a derogatory term for Negroes. His originality consisted in taking the phrase "All Coons Look Alike To Me" as the title of his song. It became a popular racial joke, given an extra flavor of insult since it was the claim of a colored man himself. Hogan first made his reputation as a showman performing the song, but he later said he regretted having written it, and apologized for it in interviews for the rest of his life.

Featured in the olio of the Black Patti show, Hogan also served as stage manager the winter of 1898. His first big solo role was in Dunbar and Cook's *Clorindy,* but after starring for the summer in the operetta, he returned to the Black Patti Troubadours for another season as the company's leading man. Hogan was a skillful performer and composer of a very popular song, and his career seemed to be going well until one evening in New Orleans, when his self-confidence was suddenly shattered. He had finished his stint in the theater for the night and went to the box office to sign for a cash advance on his salary, a privilege frequently given him by the Black Patti. Unable to find either Voelckel or Nolan, Patti's managers who would countersign his salary claim, Hogan approached the white man in the box office, a stranger who managed the local theater. Hogan's request seemed so preposterous that the box office attendant laughed at him, then became abusive when Hogan insisted. As Hogan told his friend Tom Fletcher,

> *The man I met started cursing at me and raised his fist but I beat him to the punch and knocked him down. Before anything else could happen Mr. Nolan arrived and broke up the scrap. He hid me away until that night, then got me out of town. I didn't get myself together again until I was in Australia with my own company.*

Hogan tried to leave the Patti show immediately, advertising his own production of *The King of Coontown* in the February 25, 1899 *Dramatic Mirror.* But without backers or sufficient capital, he gave up this plan and went back to the Troubadours, saving money for what he considered his "escape." In May, 1899, he left the United States to tour Hawaii, Australia, and New Zealand. After a year in which he regained his courage, he placed a series of advertisements in the *Dramatic Mirror* triumphantly proclaiming his command performance before the King of Hawaii, his eleven week tour in Honolulu, and his decision to purchase property in Hawaii for "a permanent home." In July, 1900, he was back in New York to star in Cook and Dunbar's second operetta, *Jes Lak White Folks.*

The career of the Negro entertainer Bob Cole parallels most closely that of George Walker's. Like Walker, Cole never liked to appear without a partner, at first playing the piano and singing with Billy Johnson, then teaming up with J. Rosamond Johnson, the song writer, Billy's brother. Robert A. Cole was born in Athens, Georgia, in 1868, the son of a "carpetbagger" politician. Cole went to Atlanta University for a short time, until his desire to be a playwright and composer brought him to Chicago and New York. His first songs, "Parthenia Takin' Liken' to a Coon" and "In Skin Bone Alley," were printed by the Chicago publisher Will Rossiter, who heard Cole sing in a South Side Chicago cabaret. A few years later, his songs only a fair success, Cole joined Sam T. Jack's *Creole Show,* playing comedy roles. After he married Stella Wiley, a young dancer with the *Creole Show,* they came to New York for a job at Worth's Museum, in the Tenderloin, at Sixth Avenue and 30th Street. In previous years Worth's Museum had housed fire and sword eaters, Siamese twins, two-headed calves, and the pickled head of President Garfield's assassin, but in 1895 it had moved opposite the Haymarket, the dance hall famous for its private cubicles behind the public dance floor, where hasty recitals of the cancan and hoochy-cooch were given to "heavy-spenders."

With an "All Star Stock Company" at Worth's Museum, Cole organized a revue made up of young Negro vaudevillians: Billy and Willie Farrell, the cake-walk dancers, Tom Brown, Fred Pifer, Mamie Flowers, Billy Johnson, Mattie Wilkes, Gussie L. Davis, Will Proctor, and Stella Wiley, among others. The Museum offered "dramatic training" to its fifteen member company, with

Robert Cole   Rosamond Johnson

Cole serving as director, playwright, and stage manager. Their shows were popular with Tenderloin clients, who dropped in to watch a comedy routine or hear a sentimental ballad, and Cole asked the owner of the Museum for a raise. When he was refused, Cole looked around for another job.

Hearing of the young man's skill and talent, Dick Jones approached him with a proposition: would Cole like to write and produce a show for Madame Sissieretta Jones? In 1896 not many other offers to a Negro entertainer looked so good. Cole not only wrote the hour-long farce, "Jolly Coon-ey Island," for the Black Patti, but he also brought with him the second part of the program, the vaudeville olio acts. Dick Jones had contacted the right man. When Bob Cole and Stella Wiley left Worth's Museum, they took with them most of the "All-Star Stock Company" who formed the nucleus of the first Black Patti Troubadours.

The first tour of the Troubadours so amply repaid the investments of its backers that Bob Cole repeated the action that had cost him his last job. He asked for a raise. Again, to his amazement, he was refused, and when he threatened to leave the company, his bluff was called. Cole haughtily gathered his faithful troupe—and the musical score for "Jolly Coon-ey Island"—and departed. Before he could get far the managers had him put into prison, not because they felt the show couldn't go on without him, but because they claimed the rights to the score of the musical farce. After weeks of accusations and emotional exchanges, the complicated business was settled out of court. The Black Patti kept the sketch, and Bob Cole pocketed a considerable sum of money.

Cole wasn't at a loss for material. He and Billy Johnson had another comedy, *A Trip to Coontown,* which they wrote with Sam Corker, Jr., the summer of 1897. In between some vaudeville appearances at Proctor's Music Hall, Cole and Johnson cast and rehearsed the new show, and it opened on September 27, 1897, at South Amboy, New Jersey. *A Trip to Coontown* was the first show of its kind to be written, produced, and owned by Negroes. It was a musical farce with vaudeville attractions, following the pattern established in the early years of American musical comedy. Cole and Johnson's play featured Cole in the comic character "Willie Wayside," a tramp who wore baggy trousers and a funny nose and found himself the target of practical jokes throughout the evening. Cole had none of the pretentions of the Black Patti, nor any of Hogan's personal insecurities. Like George Walker, he apparently had no difficulty accepting the standard caricatured Negro roles. With *A Trip to Coontown,* Cole and Johnson toured the country for years.

Williams and Walker's *A Lucky Coon* held its own in the wake of the Black Patti Troubadours and *A Trip to Coontown.* In June, 1899, Bert and George had finished a successful first season and were back in New York. They had made money for Hurtig and Seamon, so they began preparations for another musical.

When not in rehearsals, Walker embellished their reputation with publicity stunts like their purchase of a new-fangled automobile, a locomobile, in which he and Williams took ostentatious trips to Coney Island, searching for "summer breezes." On June 22, 1899, Walker got his name in the papers with an even larger announcement—his marriage to Ada Overton. The columnists reported,

> George Walker, of Williams and Walker, was married on Thursday evening to Ada Overton, a dusky belle, who is the soubrette of the Williams and Walker Company. The ceremony was performed by the Reverend Hutchins C. Bishop of St. Philips' Episcopal Church. An elaborate dinner was served in the apartments which will be the future home of the bride and groom. Bert Williams was ill and unable to be present, but he sent a handsome gift. Hurtig and Seamon gave George Walker a diamond-studded charm, and Ada Overton Walker a diamond necklace. The other presents were numerous and pretty.

Marriage didn't end Walker's jaunts about town. He and Williams continued to stroll through the Tenderloin, talking in the crowded bars with friends under the large, slowly moving fans that vainly attempted to cool New York during the summer heat. Williams would tell stories in his lazy drawl, and he and Walker would soon be surrounded by listeners, until Walker would get tired of the place, settle the bill, take his straw hat from the rack, and move Williams along to the next cafe. They usually finished the evening at Marshall's Restaurant on Fifty-third Street, where a number of theatrical performers congregated. According to legend, Lillian Russell, Diamond Jim Brady, Anna Held, Florenz Ziegfeld, and Weber and Fields sat and talked for hours at Marshall's, encouraged by the restaurant management to take "unlimited extended leisure." James Weldon Johnson, the Negro writer, has reminisced about evenings there, when a group of show people gathered around Bert Williams' table to listen to him tell in a dry, slow voice how Mr. Carter, the owner of Carter's Little Liver Pills, had met him in a bar at Thirtieth Street and Sixth Avenue, and suggested that he incorporate into one of the songs he was singing a verse advertising Carter's Little Liver Pills. Carter even furnished a few rough lines rhyming rocks and rills with the liver pills. Williams at his end of the bar called to Walker at the other end and asked him what he thought of the idea. Walker had Carter repeat the doggerel several times, then after an elaborate exchange of repetition with Williams, pronounced the idea to be a good one. It would cost Mr. Carter three hundred dollars. Carter had not quite expected that, but there was nothing for him to do except agree, if he wanted to do business. Walker returned to his cronies at the other end of the bar; Carter waited around for a few minutes and finally spoke again to Williams about the verse. Bert called George and reluctantly George turned away from his friends.

Williams asked if he had composed a verse yet. For a moment George was vague, but suddenly he supplied a first line. Bert thought a moment, then came up with a second line, Walker a third and together they spoke a last one. Then, very pleased with themselves, they repeated the entire verse. And again and again. It called for a drink for the house on Bert Williams; then one on George Walker. Carter, keeping his end of the deal, handed over the three hundred dollars—they had sold him his own verse.

The next Williams and Walker show, *The Policy Players,* opened in October, 1899. It was another vaudeville farce, and the most realistic newspaper critic might well have been the anonymous reviewer who gave praise to "the bud if not the flower of the colored profession." Probably the show was most warmly received when it toured Lawrence, Kansas, Walker's home town. After the one-night stand there in the Bowersock Opera House, the president of the Twentieth Century Club came onstage and gave Walker a silver loving cup "in appreciation of the prominence George Walker has brought to the town by becoming so successful." Hurtig and Seamon felt they were backing a winner, and at the beginning of the summer, 1900, when *The Policy Players* had completed its tour, they signed "The Two Real Coons" to another year under their management.

It started out to be a very pleasant summer. Williams and Walker stayed in New York City, appearing in July and August at Proctor's Theater in a vaudeville sketch to try out some new ideas for their next show. The *Dramatic Mirror* thought they seemed "to be endeavoring to get as far away as possible from the conventional Sixth Avenue coon type, and in this act they have gone the limit, geographically. The skit closes with a moonlit African jungle scene, as Walker, dressed in the negligee costume of a dusky female savage, and his partner, attired after the fashion of a male warrior, hop about the stage in a realistic aboriginal manner."

When not at work Bert and George often met Ernest Hogan, who was currently appearing at the Cherry Blossom Theater in Dunbar and Cook's second operetta, *Jes Lak White Folks*. Hogan was older than either Williams or Walker, and had achieved greater popular success, but the three men shared a deep involvement in the theater. Hogan told them about his disasterous experiences touring in the South and cautioned Bert and George about their enthusiastic belief that an apparently unlimited opportunity stretched before them. Hogan preferred reminiscing about Hawaii, a place where he felt prejudice didn't exist, and he contemptuously quoted the racial intolerance of vaudevillians like Miss Artie Hall, the white "Original Georgia Coon Shouter," who boasted in her act that she was "given a ginger ale supper by the Harriet Beecher Stowe Society. They said I was a shining example of what a coon could do if she wuz only left alone."

Williams and Walker agreed that conditions weren't perfect, but they insisted that things were getting better all the time. They saw improvement in their own situation; Hogan himself was starring in Dunbar and Cook's second operetta; the Black Patti Troubadours were still drawing crowds; Cole and Johnson were touring with *A Trip to Coontown;* and young Negro entertainers like Billy Kersands were billed in new shows like Isham's *King Rastus.* Hogan disagreed. He knew he had only been back from Hawaii a few months and was still jittery about being in America, but he felt something in the air. His intuition was correct.

The evening of August 15, 1900, shortly before 11 p.m., throughout the West Side of New York City, from Broadway west to Ninth Avenue, in all the side streets between Twenty-eighth and Forty-second, mobs of whites brutally assaulted every Negro they could find. The cause of the riot was a murder three days before, when a Negro named Arthur Harris, a Tenderloin pimp, had stabbed a vice squad patrolman to death. The police department was enraged;

the killing had to be avenged immediately and the killer taken into custody. A strong hostility to the Negroes who had migrated from the South and settled on the West Side had been building up, and the murder was seized as an excuse for the police to exercise a reign of terror in their efforts to "clean the niggers out." Secret plans were laid within the precinct where the murder had been committed, and on August 15th, the night before Officer Thorpe's funeral, rioting broke out with a speed and violence that indicated skillful organization behind the scenes.

In the words of one reporter, "Negroes were baited wherever found. They were pursued, beaten, and kicked by young men, and the usual attitude of the police was to push their way through to the victims, use their clubs on them and then carry them to the police station, where the brutality was continued." At the Twentieth Precinct station house, Police Inspector Thomspon shouted at his other officers: "Club every damned nigger you see—kill them—shoot them— be brave, same as I was."

Police stopped all the streetcars running on Eighth Avenue and threw all Negroes to the crowds. Obviously respectable Negroes on their way home from long hours of work were beaten mercilessly. Defenseless men, women, and children were terrorized by the rioting mobs. Those who ran to the police for protection were thrown back into the street. The riot continued all night, finally getting out of hand when Eighth Avenue was a mass of struggling bodies, black and white. It was at the beginning of this tumult, just before midnight, when Williams and Walker finished their nightly appearance at Proctor's Theater on Fifty-eighth Street. News of the rioting downtown had not yet reached the theater.

Williams was tired and said he would return to his apartment and go to bed. Walker had made plans to meet Hogan in the Tenderloin and, all unsuspecting, boarded a downtown streetcar. The *Dramatic Mirror* described with its customary facetiousness what the Negro showmen encountered during the night mare of August 15, 1900.

> There was a genuine "hot time in the old town" last Wednesday night, when a terrible race riot occurred in New York. A policeman was murdered by a Negro, and every black man found on the street was horribly beaten. Among the victims of the mob were Ernest Hogan and George Walker, whose business compelled them to be abroad just when the riot was at its worst.

Hogan's fears had come true. A few years had intervened between "The Two Real Coons" and their unpleasant experience in Texas with the medicine show, but once again they came face to face with intense hatred and blind, unreasonable hostility. Hogan was so badly injured by the rioting mobs that he was forced to leave the cast of Dunbar's operetta. Walker escaped into a cellar and hid throughout the night. The horror and cruelty of the incident affected Bert Williams strongly. He withdrew further into himself, no longer so talkative with strangers who used to find him expanding into humorous anecdotes in his afternoons of relaxation, and definitely not so accessible to "white folks" like Mr. Carter, of the Little Liver Pills.

THE MEDICINE MAN.

Arr. by W. H. Tyers.

By Williams & Walker.

1. Do you ev – er have dat pain in your head? Do you feel nervous when you go to bed? Does your

2. I felt as sick as I could be 'Long in the year of nine-ty three, And

1097-3

pulse run up to a high de-gree? Does your bod-y feel warmer than it
ev'-ry-bo-dy had a rem-e-dy Guar-an-teed to cure in a

ought to be? You might have the col-ic, Or you might have the grip, Cause when a
minute, don't you see! Some-how I got worse and had to go to bed, They had to

man is sick he drops his low-er lip! If it's 'so-ci-a-ted with the
put ice, by the pound, on my head; They sent for a man named

burning of the hand, You need some herbs from the med-i-cine man.
Doc - tor Horn, And he had me out of bed by nine next morn.

CHORUS.

Oh, de medicine man, ... Wid de grip in his hand, ... He's in

ever-y land; When he explains a - bout your pains Your hair on end will stand! If you

feel kinder sick .... Why you better run quick, ... Go as

quick as you can, 'Cause no-body knows but the medicine man. Oh, de medicine man.

SONS OF HAM

BERT WILLIAMS was powerless to stop nightmares like the race riot of August 15, 1900, but he was working out his own way of dealing with the strain of being a Negro in the United States. He was proud, he had never considered himself a close relative of anyone from the American South, but he had learned that so far as the general public was concerned, there was only one kind of Negro, and anyone whose skin was colored was a target for the indignities of racial prejudice. Faced with what looked to him like a hopeless situation, Williams tried to minimize his encounters with intolerance and discrimination. He began to separate his public and private lives as much as he could. For the stage, he saw himself "as another person," developing a comic personality under the mask of blackface. In his private life, on the other hand, he identified himself as little as possible with the Negro people about him.

Part of Williams' detachment was a constitutional reserve; he had liked to be left alone even as a child, when he preferred watching people to doing things with them. Another reason for his feeling of exclusiveness was his West Indian birth. He was proud of his ancestry and disinclined to forget that his social background was superior to that of most Negroes he met in the theater. Besides, there has always been a certain amount of difference in the United States between West Indian and American Negroes, as the former generally feel a strong emotional pride and detachment as foreigners. But there was a definitely inexplicable quality to Williams' reserve. Although he continued a business partnership with a Negro from Kansas for sixteen years, and took some part in Negro professional organizations, he always discouraged close personal friendships. His reserve might have been the result of some deep personal humiliation he might have felt since he was making a career out of exploiting the "coon" stereotype on the stage, or it might have been that since he was forced into the professional role of a Negro, he felt he'd compensate by forgetting his racial identity as completely as possible in his private life. Whatever the reason, he was a man without many friends. Even his marriage has an aura of secrecy.

Unlike George and Ada Overton Walker, Bert and Lottie Thompson Williams did not announce their marriage to the newspapers, nor is there a record of a civil ceremony in the files of the New York Hall of Records. A few weeks after the race riot, just before the opening of the Williams and Walker musical *Sons of Ham* in September, 1900, Bert quietly announced to his partner and the entire company that he and Lottie were married. Lottie Thompson had been in the Williams and Walker company for more than two years. She had joined the cast of the *Senegambian Carnival* in 1898, when it passed through Chicago, replacing one of the girls who through sudden illness was unable to sing in *Clorindy*. Several years older than Bert, she had been born Lottie Cole in Chicago in 1866, and was a medium height, light skinned woman with a well trained, clear soprano voice and a very capable stage presence. She came into the Williams and Walker company at the end of her marriage to a Chicago businessman, Sam Thompson, and it has never been clear whether she and Thompson were legally divorced. She was in all the Williams and Walker productions, but when Bert became a star performer in the Ziegfeld Follies, she retired from the stage. Show people who remember her say that she mothered Bert, devoting herself to making his home comfortable. He was a chain smoker, and he enjoyed having her light his first cigaret for him in the morning. Lottie was a calm, domineering woman who shared Bert's social reserve. They were together for more than twenty years, without children, and she is mostly remembered for waiting up for her husband when he was late getting home from the theater. Friends who accompanied him to his front door remember Lottie's angry face, and the inevitable beginning of Bert's repentant excuse, "Now mother. . . ." Joking about Lottie's protective concern, once Bert confided to a friend that whenever he knew "mother" was going to be angry with him, he always had a manicure, because "I can always charm mother with my hands."

It is characteristic of Williams that his favorite story about his marriage showed him laughing "at his own misfortune." When *Sons of Ham* played Chicago, the newly married couple visited Lottie's family, taking her parents to spend a day at a pleasure park in the suburbs. Bert had just bought a new pair of patent leather shoes, and after walking around the park all afternoon, his feet hurt him terribly. The whole party finally boarded a crowded streetcar to return home, and Bert was forced to stand. He eased his weight from one foot to another, hoping that nobody would step on him or even come near his shoes. Finally when the crowd had thinned, he got a seat and very stealthily reached down to unbutton his shoes. With great casualness he pointed out the window and engaged Lottie's attention while he slipped "the danged things" off.

When the streetcar finally neared the neighborhood where Lottie's family lived, Bert tried to slip his feet back into the shoes. It was impossible; his feet had swollen so much that it felt to him like a difference of about five sizes. In the rush of leaving the streetcar, Lottie didn't see him hide the shoes under his coat. He helped her carefully to the sidewalk, where she started to take his arm, and at about the same moment her parents began to smile at Williams' appearance, Lottie discovered her husband in his stocking feet. She stopped short, looked at him standing ruefully before her, and joined her family—and Bert—in laughter.

Whatever the atmosphere of reserve Williams maintained for his private life, he continued in the spotlight on the stage. The new Williams and Walker show,

Sons of Ham, was ready for rehearsals in September, 1900. Jesse Shipp, who had helped write *The Policy Players,* was on hand to outline the general action and dialogue of the plot, but Bert and George ad-libbed their lines and invented stage business as they went along. The method worked fairly well. Whenever either of them hit on something particularly funny, Jesse Shipp would write it down. The first few performances of *Sons of Ham* were fairly rough, but by listening carefully to the audience's reaction and remembering the lines that got the most laughter, so that they could repeat them in subsequent performances, Williams and Walker perfected their roles.

Sons of Ham had a title that was offensive to many sensitive people, who protested against it in the newspapers until Walker tried to silence their objections by explaining that the term was respectable since it appeared in the Bible. In this musical Williams and Walker played two itinerant derelicts who stumbled into Denver, Colorado. What they were doing in the West was anybody's idea, but they were mistaken for a pair of twin brothers who were expected to return

Bert and Lottie Williams

from boarding school and claim a large family fortune. Although Ham, the father of the twins, hadn't seen his sons for many years, he readily accepted the two bums as his own children. Bert and George settled back to enjoy their fortune, but it seemed that the real twins had learned to be acrobats and gun-jugglers at the boarding school, and the bums were put on the spot. Two acts of frantic efforts to avoid exposure as phonies led to the inevitable appearance of the real sons and heirs, with the impostors' expulsion from town. Ada Overton Walker and Lottie Thompson acted and sang as Denver citizens, Jesse Shipp played Ham, and the Reese Brothers, vaudeville acrobats, were the real twins. The liveliness of the company overcame the sheer nonsense of the plot to an extent that one enthusiastic reviewer called it "good in the superlative degree." Hurtig and Seamon's property toured the country from October to May, as far West as Nebraska, for two seasons.

Little except the bare plot outline of *Sons of Ham* has survived to the present time, but on October 11, 1901, just before beginning the second season of the musical, Williams and Walker became involved in an enterprise that had much greater longevity. On that date they visited the top floor of a five story building on Broadway and made their first phonograph records.

In 1901 the recording industry was still in its infancy, and what Bert and George saw in the studio probably surprised them. Vocalists stood on soap boxes and leaned into funnels connected to receiving cylinders; three records were made simultaneously, and when they were finished, the performer rested while the reproduction machine was prepared for another session. Instrumentalists—men playing piccolos, clarinets, cornets, trombones, tubas, or pianos—were grouped on separate platforms, each different levels, according to the recording engineer's beliefs about minimum distortion. The quality of reproduction was so poor that most artists wouldn't record, since the cylinders distorted the sound so much that most acts invariably sounded terrible. Companies like Victor, Edison, and Lambert usually hired relatively unknown singers who had no reputations to lose—men like Len Spenser, Arthur Collins, Billy Murray, Steve Porter, Dan Quinn, and Roger Harding. These singers were chosen on the basis of how clearly they could enunciate the words, since the public wouldn't buy records they couldn't understand.

Williams and Walker had heard some of the early cylinders and were curious to hear how their voices would sound. In the studio of Victor Company on October 11, 1901, they first tried a duet, "I Don't Like That Face You Wear." Then Bert sang four solo songs, George three numbers by himself, and they finished the first session with another duet, "Good Morning, Carrie."

On the playback, Walker's voice sounded very thin and unsubstantial, like a cross between an Irish and a Kansas tenor. Only a suggestion of his dash and bravado lurked behind "Her Name's Miss Dinah Fair," his last solo. In contrast, Williams' voice was strong, especially spirited in "The Phrenologist Coon," a song written for him by Ernest Hogan.

Of all the men of history,
'Tis said I'se the mystery;

As conjer man I'se the king.
For I'se well versed in psychology,
Knows all about phrenology,
In ethnology I'se the thing.

George Walker, Bert Williams and Ada Overton Walker

I can tell you what you are
By feeling of your bump,
And in the mysteries of the future
I can certainly make you jump.
When I has an inspiration
All the future I can see,
I can tell you what you are and was
And what you gwine to be.

For his songs Bert had used a pianist who was a regular Victor Records accompanist, but George had insisted that his partner accompany him, and since Bert was a self-taught, fits-and-starts ragtime player, Walker was further handicapped by having no clearly defined rhythm or harmony behind him. George was disappointed in the records he had made, and since he felt the wax impression of his voice retained little of his personality, he decided he would skip any further recording sessions.

Williams was more absorbed in the sound of his own performance. It was hard to tell anything from the poor quality of the recording techniques, which could only reproduce a shouted roar, but he had practiced his songs and worked on his dialect so conscientiously that he wanted the records played over and over, comparing how he had always thought he sounded to the strained music coming from the cylinder machine. At that time theatrical stars refused to make records, contemptuous of the poor quality of the sound reproduction and afraid that people who owned their records would tire of their acts. But despite the apparent disadvantages of the new recording process, when Williams was invited to come back to the Victor studio in another month, he agreed. He was to sing into recording mechanisms for the rest of his life.

Williams' interest was justified, for as techniques improved, vocal reproductions became more faithful. Although recordings can never duplicate the full quality and presence of an artist's work, they can make him immortal. After his death in 1922, Bert Williams was still alive on the recordings he had made during his lifetime. To people interested in his art, the records from October 11, 1901, to February 24, 1922, are a source that reveal the growth and maturation of his vocal style. His records are also a fascinating survival of popular entertainment from the early years of this century, and for those listeners who aren't historians but who just want to enjoy a good funny song, there are Williams' renditions of "Nobody," "I'm Goin' To Quit on Saturday," "My Landlady," "10 Little Bottles". . . The list goes on for scores of titles, and all of them sold well.

There were many recording sessions for Bert Williams, but his first one with Walker is unique; Bert was so appalled at how he sounded playing ragtime accompaniments that he never went near a piano again when a recording horn was pointed his way. Walker shook his head after the first recording session. He announced he was finished with the whole tiresome business. He was to overcome his reluctance about five years later to record the song "Pretty Desdemone" for Columbia Company, but in 1901 he was much more eager to begin the second season of *Sons of Ham.*

Introduced and Featured by the Two Real Coons, Williams & Walker.

Good Morning Carrie!

THE STARS KNOW THIS IS A GOOD SONG.

WILLIAMS & WALKER.

Words by
R. C. McPHERSON

Music by
SMITH & BOWMAN

50¢

PUBLISHED BY
Windsor Music Co.
266-268 WABASH AVE., CHICAGO.
41 W. 28th ST. NEW YORK.
CANADA MUSIC CO.,   WICKINS & CO.,
1450 QUEEN ST. W. TORONTO, CAN.   41 N. BOND ST. LONDON, ENG.

GOOD MORNING CARRIE!

Words by R. C. McPHERSON.

Music by SMITH & BOWMAN.

1. In sun - ny South Car - 'li - na lives an old aunt Di - nah And her daughter named Car - o -
2. There's dusk - y suit - ers plen - ty that would take my Car-rie from me, But she's promised to be on - ly

line. She's winsome cute and air - y, her folks they call her Car - rie, I hope some day, that she'll be
mine. With ten - der songs of woo-ing like the tur - tle dove a coo - ing, They ser - en - ade my Car - o -

mine.   To   meet her ev - 'ry   ev - 'ning when the   stars are bright-ly beam-ing Brings
line.   We'll be   wed - ded   soon thats   cer - tain   and   some hearts will be   a   hurt - in'   When

joy and pleas-ure to my heart so   lone,   In the light of ear - ly dawn   with my
budding leaves and flow - ers   tell 'tis   spring,   There'll   be   no great dis - play   but

mf

ban - jo   on   my arm,   I   a - wake her   from   her slum - ber   with this   song:
on   our   wed - ding day,   We'll   ask   the folks   a - round   to   kind - ly   sing:

poco rit.

Good Morning Carrie! 3-2.

Good morning Car - rie..... how you do this morn - ing..... Was you dream - ing

Repeat Chorus only in 2nd verse.

'bout me..... my pret - ty maid,.............. Say look here Car - rie..... when we gwine to

mar - ry...... Long spring time hon ey,..... good morn-ing babe......... Good morning ...

Good Morning Carrie! 3-3.

IN DAHOMEY

I N THE SUMMER of 1902, when *Sons of Ham* had finished its second
tour, Williams and Walker began to prepare what they hoped would be
the biggest, most successful Negro show ever produced in America. Hurtig
and Seamon were willing to put up fifteen thousand dollars, at that time
a considerable sum to spend on a musical. George and Bert asked Jesse Shipp
to help with the new production before deciding also to call in Will Marion
Cook and Paul Dunbar for assistance with the music and lyrics.

Walker had had a brainstorm: he proposed that they build the new show
around the African elements in the American Negro background, although he
had confused ideas about where the line was to be drawn around "African."
Soon he was to claim that

> *the departure from what was popularly known as the American
> "darky" ragtime limitations to native African characteristics has
> helped greatly to increase the value of the blackface performer on
> the American stage.*

> *Managers gave little credit to the ability of black people on the stage
> before the native African element was introduced. All that was ex-
> pected of a colored performer was singing, dancing, and a little story
> telling, but as for acting, no one credited a black person with the
> ability to act.*

Walker may have felt he was a great innovator, but what he accomplished
was really just a more elaborately mounted vaudeville farce. In a way he was restricted by the theatrical standards of his time. Musical comedy was still young
and relatively unformed at the start of the twentieth century, certainly not en-
couraging authentic racial statements. Walker was further hampered by his own
personal limitations, however. He may have liked to think of himself as a coura-
geous pioneer, but rather than developing a thoughtful conception of "native
African characteristics," what he actually produced was closer to a superficial
theatrical novelty. He had only the vaguest notions about Africa and was totally
without interest in a strong identification with the country. Operating as a
shrewd business man, Walker realized that the public had had enough plantation

shows in the previous century. He wanted to try something new, looking forward to increased box office sales as much as increased respect for the Negro entertainer. The new production was to be named *In Dahomey,* after the one time Williams and Walker had brushed against real Africans in the San Francisco Exposition many years before.

In their first sessions trying to write the show it became clear that neither Williams, Walker, nor Jesse Shipp knew much about Dahomey. It seemed wiser not to have all the action take place in Africa, because their imagination and courage stretched a little thin over three acts and a cast of fifty people. The bare outline of the plot they finally constructed certainly came a long way from the lofty intentions Walker had announced to the press. Considering the popularity that *In Dahomey* was to have with audiences for years, its story seems scarcely strong enough to support the care Williams and Walker lavished on its production.

They decided to have the action start first in America, then move to Africa, and with this inspiration the ideas tumbled on helter-skelter. It was very much on the order of the farce comedy *Sons of Ham.* A group of unscrupulous business men in Boston proposed to colonize some land in Africa as a haven for oppressed Negroes, sending "Rareback Pinkerton" (George Walker) down to Florida to persuade a wealthy but senile Negro to finance the scheme. "Shylock Homestead" (Bert Williams), a happy simpleton who beat a drum in a Salvation Army Band, went to Florida with the crooks, unknowingly being used as a dupe by Rareback in the presentation of the scheme. When businessmen learned that Shylock was the heir to the great Florida fortune, Rareback dazzled him by offers of friendship, just so that he would be appointed trustee to the estate. In possession of Shylock's money, Rareback blossomed in glorious clothes and became the leader of Florida and Dahomey society, while Shylock remained the bumpkin with a blind faith in his friend's goodness. Finally after Rareback made such a preposterous demand for money that Shylock found the strength to refuse, the simpleton signed over the remainder of his inheritance to the Dahomey colony.

The biggest advantage of the plot was that large crowds of singers and dancers could be on stage at all times. The businessman's meeting, the Salvation Army band members, the grand parties and society balls in Florida, the entire Dahomian village, did more than fill up space with colorful costumes and backdrop scenery. The music and lyrics Cook and Dunbar wrote for the show had a lively appeal, and Walker saw to it that "when there is any singing to be done, and it is indulged in every five minutes, there is always a good sized crowd on hand to swell the harmony."

In Dahomey might not have given audiences any greater insight into African culture, but it proved so popular that just before Easter, 1903, after several months on the road, Williams and Walker found themselves achieving something that they both had dreamed about since they entered show business. They were booked into the New York Theater at Fifty-ninth Street and Broadway. Williams told an interviewer what it meant to them:

The way we've aimed for Broadway and just missed it in the past seven years would make you cry. We'd get our bearings, take a good running start and—land in a Third Avenue theater. Then we'd measure the distance again and think we'd struck the right avenue at last—only to be stalled in a West Thirty-fourth Street music hall with the whole stunt to do all over again. We'd get near enough to hear the Broadway audiences applaud sometimes, but it was someone else they were applauding. I used to be tempted to beg for a fifteen dollar job in a chorus just for one week so as to be able to say I'd been on Broadway once.

With *In Dahomey,* Bert Williams was recognized as one of the leading comedians in the country. In previous Williams and Walker shows he had grown into his characterization until his timing and pantomime were developed to the point where "all he had to do was look at the audience and it went into spasms promptly." As usual, Walker was quick to explain to the press that "My partner, Mr. Williams, is the first man that I know of in our race to attempt to delineate a darky in a perfectly natural way, and I think much of his success is due to this fact."

Williams' comic role had been strengthened by a new song, "Jonah Man," which he wrote with Alex Rogers during the summer of 1900. The words chronicled the hard times, completely unavoidable, encountered by an unlucky "Jonah Man." With the song, Bert's basic stage character, "the fellow who is the goat," emerged clearly, and "Jonah Man" took the place of "I Don't Want No Cheap Man," the number that had been Bert's theme song ever since he'd introduced it with Hydes' Comedians.

My luck started when I was born,
Leas' so the old folks say.
Dat same hard luck's been my bes' frien'
To dis vary day.
When I was young, Mama's friends—to find a name they tried.
They named me after Papa—and de same day papa died, Fo'—

(Chorus)
I'm a Jonah, I'm a Jonah Man,
My family for many years would look at me
And den shed tears.
Why I am dis Jonah
I sho' can't understand,
But I'm a good substantial, full-fledged
Real, first-class Jonah Man.

Shortly after Williams' opening on Broadway, *Theater Magazine,* a journal with exacting standards, called him "a vastly funnier man than any white comedian now on the American stage."

As well as a personal success for Williams, *In Dahomey* brought his partnership with Walker to what was probably its greatest triumph—the show's tour of England in 1903–1904. On April 28, 1903, the entire *In Dahomey* company

WILLIAMS AND WALKER'S

CROWNING   *BERT WILLIAMS*   *GEO WALKER*   SUCCESS

I'M A JONAH MAN

SUNG
AT EVERY PERFOR-
MANCE OF THEIR
LATEST MUSICAL
PRODUCTION
"IN DAHOMEY"

WORDS
AND
MUSIC
BY
ALEX. ROGERS

M. WITMARK & SONS

I'm A Jonah Man.

by ALEX ROGERS.

1. My hard luck start-ed when I was born leas'__ so the old folks say. Dat__ same hard luck been__ my be's fren' up__
2. A fren' of mine gave me a six months__ meal tick-et one day. He__ said it wont do__ me no good I've__
3. My broth-er once walked down the street and__ fell in a coal hole. He__ sued the man that__ owned the place and__

5163 - 3

to dis ver - y day.   When I was young my__
got to go a - way.   I__ thanked him as my__
got ten - thou - sand cold.   I__ fig - ured this was__

mam - ma's frens to__ find a name they tried.   They
heart wid joy and__ grat - i - tude did bound.   But
eas - y so I__ jumped in the same coal hole.   Broke

named me af - ter Pa - pa and the__ same day Pa - pa died.   For
when I reached the res - tau - rant the__ place he'd just burned down.   For
both my legs and the Judge give me one__ year for steal - in' coal.   For

I'm A Jonah Man. 5163 - 3

CHORUS.

I'm a Jo - nah, I'm a Jo - nah man. My
I'm a Jo - nah, I'm a Jo - nah man. It
I'm a Jo - nah, I'm a Jo - nah man. If it

fam - i - ly for man - y years would look on me and then shed tears,
sounds just like that old old tale But some-times I feel like a whale,
rained down coin I hope to choke I b'lieve I'd have a par-a-let-ic stroke,

Why am I dis Jo - nah I sho' cant un-der-stand, But I'm a
Why am I dis Jo - nah I sho' cant un-der-stand, But I'm a
Why am I dis Jo - nah I sho' cant un-der-stand, But I'm a

good sub-stan - tial full fledged real first class Jo - nah man.
good sub-stan - tial full fledged real first class Jo - nah man.
good sub-stan - tial full fledged real first class Jo - nah man.

I'm A Jonah Man. 5163-3

sailed to London on the S.S. Urania, booked to open at the Shaftesbury Theater. Worrying about the memory of his first unsuccessful appearance on the London music hall stage in 1897, Williams found himself listening to the many "friends and friendly enemies" who gave advice on how to make a hit before English audiences. Finally the ultimate suggestion was offered: Bert was told he shouldn't appear in cork.

> *At first I thought that they meant Cork, Ireland, but they soon assured me that to blacken my face with burnt cork would be to puzzle the English theater goers, who wouldn't "get me." For about ten minutes they had me going, but all of a sudden I got sort of bullish myself and stopped listening to suggestions.*

For the first month's performances, *In Dahomey* played to appreciative but not exceptionally enthusiastic crowds. It was not until June 23, 1903, that the show became a hit. The event that made the difference was the command performance at Buckingham Palace celebrating the birthday of the young Prince of Wales.

For this gala party, the scenery and costumes for the show were sent to the Palace and a theater especially erected in the Palace gardens. The stage, completely furnished with galleries and props, faced the Palace across a vast lawn. There were chairs for the King and Queen, but the rest of the audience sat on the grass. Everything was prepared for the actors; they had only to make up and dress to go onstage. To suit the requirements of a children's entertainment, the show had been slightly modified and abridged, since as a London newspaper said, the performance was "nominally given for the amusement of little Prince Edward," but both children and adults thought it a great hit. Inspired by the generous applause, the actors performed with great spirit and confidence. The children at the party seemed especially fond of Bert's song, "Jonah Man," but he had wondered whether it would be acceptable for him to sing "Evah Darkey is a King" before King Edward VII and the royal family. Bert included the song as usual in the show, and encountered no apparent hard feelings.

> *Evah darkey is a king!*
> *Royalty is jes' de ting.*
> *If yo' social life's a bungle,*
> *Jes yo' go back to yo' jungle,*
> *And remember dat your daddy was a king.*

After the command performance, *In Dahomey* became the most popular musical show in London. Crowds flocked to the Shaftesbury Theater and after the final curtain, men like the Duke of Connaught, Kennedy Cox, and Cavendish Morton took Williams to their clubs and homes for dinner and conversation. The cakewalk that Jesse Shipp had written into the play especially for its English performance was a special hit, and Dan and Minnie Washington, Lavinia Gaston and Richard Covers, as well as Ada, George, Bert, and Lottie, were featured in the dance, with the prize cake awarded by audience applause. George Walker even claimed that his cakewalk strut was so much admired by the Queen that she asked especially for his photograph.

After several months in London, the Dahomey company toured England and Scotland, playing in Hull, Bristol, Newcastle, Sheffield, Manchester, Edinburgh, and Glasgow. It was at this time that Bert got to satisfy one of his social ambitions; he joined a lodge in the Masonic Order. Williams could have joined a Negro Masonic Lodge in the United States, but instead he decided to take advantage of the lack of a color bar in Great Britain. He took the first degree of the ceremony at the Waverly Lodge Number 597, St. Andrew's Chapter in Edinburgh, then he traveled with *In Dahomey* to Glasgow and Manchester. When the time came for him to take the second degree, the *In Dahomey* company was leaving Manchester, but a special dispensation was granted and Bert took his second degree early the morning of his departure. A month later he returned to Edinburgh for a third and final degree of his initiation. He was recognized as a full fledged member of the International Masonic organization, enthusiastically welcomed by his Scottish and English Masonic brothers, even if the branch of the organization in America had not yet offered its congratulations.

After more than a year away from the United States, the Williams and Walker company returned to New York to open in August, 1904, at the Grand Opera House, with *In Dahomey*. If Bert missed the praise and conversation with English fans or the fellowship of the Edinburgh Masons at the Waverly Lodge, he and George did not lack for a "very cordial reception" from American Theater managers and audiences. *In Dahomey* toured the country for forty weeks, until June, 1905, traveling as far west as Portland and San Francisco, as far south as St. Louis. The show made $64,000, more than four times Hurtig and Seamon's original investment. The team of Williams and Walker seemed solidly established in popular show business; they lent their name to a Glee Club which appeared in vaudeville, a singing group made up of chorus members from the *In Dahomey* company. A second *In Dahomey* troupe sailed to England, headed by Dan Avery and Charley Hart, two young Negro entertainers who were imitating Williams and Walker.

But back again in America, Williams and Walker found their place in society was made very clear. The highest honor paid to their company after their return was an invitation for the "sixteen refined young Afro-Americans" making up the Williams and Walker Glee Club to sing at a garden party given by Booker T. Washington at his summer home in South Weymouth.

THE FORTUNE TELLING MAN.

By WILLIAMS & WALKER.

Moderato.

1. In an old big house, jes' as
2. A man by name of Rice came to
3. The ve - ry next night, jes' be -

qui - et as a mouse, I sits an' 'casionly reads a - bout old Mars, _____ An'
see me once or twice, To tell me of his chick-ens' dis - con - tents, _____ He
fore I lit de light, A mon-strous look-ing man came to my door, _____ He

in the dead of night, with - out a speck of light, I
locked de house door, made sure it was se - cure, But his
said he'd had a dream, an aw - ful thing he'd seen, A

CHORUS.

I am dat for - tune - tell - ing man,

Dars no kind of dreams dat I can't un - der - stand,

I can tell your fu - ture by look-ing in de hand,_____ Cause

I_____ am dat for-tune-tell-ing man._____ man._____

SELECTIONS FROM
WILLIAMS & WALKER'S
MUSICAL COMEDY SUCCESS

Bandana Land

DIRECTION
F. RAY COMSTOCK

BOOK & LYRICS BY
J. A. SHIPP
AND
ALEX ROGERS
MUSIC BY
WILL MARION COOK
INTERPOLATIONS BY
BERT A. WILLIAMS

THE
GOTHAM-ATTUCKS
MUSIC COMPANY (INC)
"THE HOUSE OF MELODY"
50 W. 29th ST. N.Y. CITY

BON BON BUDDY

AFTER *In Dahomey,* which entertained thousands of people from 1902 to 1905, Williams and Walker looked forward to a long career on the popular stage. They had worked out a musical comedy format that appealed to their audiences: highly fanciful locales, the well trained voices of a large chorus, starring roles for Ada Overton Walker, whose charm and appeal were growing steadily, and a whole evening of laughs before the clowning, hard-luck simpleton, Williams, finally got wise to the fast talking dandy, Walker. In George's mind the formula was set and good for many more shows. He began to plan their next production, and his imagination expanded as he developed his ideas. The new show would double the magnificence of *In Dahomey.* It was to have a cast of 125 people, and because it was going to be "totally African," live jungle animals would have to be purchased. Williams was willing to go along with the idea for expanding the cast, but he drew the line at hiring tigers and giraffes. He argued with his stubborn partner, and finally they reached a compromise; they would buy live camels, but contortionists and acrobats would be costumed to imitate the other animals.

The disagreement over casting was the least of their business worries, however. When Walker approached Hurtig and Seamon for the sum of thirty-thousand dollars, the amount he had figured would cover expenses, the managers flatly turned him down. This was double what *In Dahomey* had cost them. They didn't think they could book the new show into first class theaters, where the higher admission prices would guarantee sufficient return on their investment. Walker left their offices angry but not defeated. He had always been proud of his ability to manage business matters, and now before him was the biggest challenge he had ever faced. *In Dahomey* had done well, but an all-Negro show was still a risky investment. Was he a good enough salesman to sell his idea to another backer?

Rehearsals were postponed while he scurried around New York, insisting, cajoling, persuading. Finally he contacted Melville B. Raymond, of the Klaw and Erlanger syndicate of theater owners, who agreed to put up the money. Rehearsals were resumed, and in the last week of February, 1908, *In Abyssinia* opened at the Majestic Theater on Columbus Circle and Fifty-eighth Street.

When It's All Goin' Out, And Nothin' Comin' In.

Words revised by James W. Johnson.

Words & Music by Williams & Walker.

Moderato.

1. Mon-ey is de root of e - vil, No mat-ter where you hap-pen to go; But no-bod-y has an-y ob-jec - -tions to de root; now ain't dat so? You

2. Had my share of dis world's tri - -als, No bod - y knows how hard I have tried; To keep my lit - tle boat from sink - in' An' to bat - tle wid de tide. You

know how it is wid mon-ey, How it makes you feel at
know when you've got yo' mon-ey, You kin ea-sy keep a-

ease, De world puts on a big broad smile, An' yo'
float, De stream is smooth an' all yo' friends, Tries to

friends am as thick as bees. But, Oh! _____ When yo' mon-ey is
help you to row yo' boat. But, Oh! _____ When yo' mon-ey is

run nin' low, An' you'se cling-ing to a sol-i-ta-ry
run nin' low, An' de stream gits rough an' things look might-y

dime,   Yo'   cred - i - tors   are num'- rous   an'   yo'
blue;   Yo'   look a round   for help an'   find   each

friends are   few,   Oh!   dat am de   aw - ful   time.
of   yo' friends, Is   pad dlin' his own   ca - noe.

poco rit.

CHORUS.

Dat am de time,_____   Oh!   dat am de time_____

— When it's   all go-in' out an'   noth -in' com -in' in,

Dat am de time when de troubles be gin; Money's git-tin' low

Peo-ple say: "I told you so;" And you

can't bor-row a pen-ny from an-y of yo' kin An' it's

all go-in' out an' noth-in' com in' in.

An immediate success, *In Abyssinia* was another *In Dahomey,* with a bigger cast and more lavish stage decorations. The opening scenery—a mountain pass with a real waterfall in the background—was so elaborate that Williams and Walker waited until the middle of the first act to come onstage, giving the audience enough time to admire the set. But once they appeared, one or both of them was rarely absent, clowning together, singing alone or with the chorus, carrying along the unsubstantial plot. Their comedy routines grew increasingly more relaxed and spontaneous; some jokes were made up on the spur of the moment, others carried along from one evening to the next. Williams had an excellent memory for laugh lines. He kept the remarks which got the most response from the audience in his routines and dropped the "clinkers."

Walker was more of a cut-up. In his bright fancy jackets and bell-bottom trousers, or bold checked suits, he cavorted around the stage, always in motion. His songs were struts of joy, impudent statements of his own talent, like the egotistical shout, "It's Hard to Find a King Like Me." Unlike Williams, Walker played himself, the ambitious hustler and wise guy, at his best when delivering streams of glib, fast talk. In stark contrast to George's noisy ranting, Bert's simple tag lines brought roars of laughter from the surprised audience. The two men were excellent foils for one another, their performances completely disguising the fact that off the stage they were not very close anymore.

Harrison Smith, a Negro song writer who knew Williams and Walker, once observed that "there was as much difference between Bert and George as distance between the Atlantic and Pacific Oceans." They were temperamentally opposite, and perhaps the basic contrast in their personalities was one of the reasons they could establish such contrasting characterizations on the stage. In their early years together they had been brought closer by the determination they both shared to gain recognition in show business. They felt that the best way to help establish their reputations was to be seen together in cafes and restaurants, and after their nightly performances in *Senegambian Carnival* or *A Lucky Coon,* they would stroll out the stage door arm in arm and climb into a waiting hansom cab. But as they prospered, they didn't have to appear such close friends. Moreover, their incompatibility of tastes and interests grew with prosperity until they became another of the famous show business teams, like McIntyre and Heath, who worked splendidly on stage but rarely met off it. When *Abyssinia* was in rehearsal, Williams didn't participate until shortly before the opening performance, letting Walker settle the production details. Alex Rogers came over to Bert's apartment every few days to keep him informed about the progress of the show, but it wasn't until the first dress rehearsal that Williams came to the theater. He and Walker then clowned through their roles, so that Bert first saw what the rest of the company was doing only a day or two before the public got to judge the show.

Out of the theater, Williams had few encounters with his partner. Preferring to shun interviewers and businessmen, he spent his time with small groups of friends in a quiet Harlem bar, or stayed at home with Lottie and read in his extensive book collection. He was skeptical of the flattery that was showered on him when he was off the stage, and suspected ulterior motives in the strangers who claimed his time or attention. He preferred not to be bothered. Once a week he rode to a barbershop in Brooklyn to get a haircut and a manicure, staying the afternoon to swap stories with "Brownie" the barber and theatrical people like Jesse Shipp, Alex Rogers, and Billy Johnson, who also frequented the shop. Bert's big outings were on Sunday, when he played baseball at the Bronx Oval, at 166th Street and Boulevard Avenue. He was captain of the Williams and Walker company team, with Louis Mitchell, "Bass" Foster, Jesse Shipp, Sam Cook, and Will Chapelle the star members. Walker never came out to play in the games. He scoffed that baseball uniforms were poorly tailored.

Besides, Walker wanted to stay closer to Broadway. Young Negro singers and dancers who had just come to New York with the small touring shows hoping to "make the big time" found that Walker enjoyed talking to them, advising them on their careers, and treating them to a drink or a meal. Entertainers, theatrical agents, and enthusiastic fans were always around to help him discuss his schemes for future glory, both for himself and all American colored-people. George was aggressively determined in business matters. Williams later described him as

> *suave; one of those oily fellows, and so persistent. Walker used to insist on having things decided his way—OUR way. In a business deal where the other party decided against us, I was usually willing to consider it settled rather than argue. Not so with Walker. He would talk on and on. "Arguing," he called it, and little by little the other side would begin to be convinced. Eventually you would have to believe that Walker was right. He had the methods of a diplomatist.*

Walker belonged to the school of showmen who believed that their lives should be one endless performance. Off the stage he was not only the shrewd opportunist, forever involved in business deals, but also he kept up the part of the extravagantly dressed dandy. As a friend said, he was a "man just born for clothes." He spent more hours with his tailor than he spent with his wife. Suits were made for him by the dozen, and he always had four or five fittings before he was satisfied with the way they looked. He bought the latest style and nothing but the best of everything, particularly addicted to light colored suits, big soft handkerchiefs that rested in his jacket pocket, high white collars, large silk patterned ties, and bright roses or carnations pinned carefully in his button-hole. He dressed to please himself and impress the public—and help him win the favors of pretty young showgirls. His wife Ada Overton was beautiful and genuinely talented, but Walker liked variety in love. His affairs were legendary: vivacious girls from the chorus line, like Jeanette Foster, later nicknamed the "Chocolate Drop Venus," and a score of others, most notorious of whom was Eva Tanguay, the white singer and dancer, the "I Don't Care" girl, who shared vaudeville billing with Williams and Walker at the Colonial Theater in the summer of 1908. She welcomed Walker in her dressingroom after the show, then left the theater with him to attend parties that lasted through the morning hours.

Relishing his celebrity status, George Walker still found time to be a leader in Negro show business. The success of the Williams and Walker productions,

I May Be Crazy, But I Ain't No Fool

Words and Music
By ALEX ROGERS

thy _____ You've heard what they __ hand farm - er folks well
cru - el _____ I think that pis - tols will be best" his
too, _____ So Lu she 'vised __ us both to jump off

that ain't one, __ two, three, With the fish - tales and the
sec - onds said __ "they will." Oh, yes, re - vol - vers
Brook - lyn Bridge next day; And the one that got back

ten.

gold bricks that they try to hand __ to me.
will just suit our friend there, "Buff' - lo Bill." _____
to her first, she'd mar - ry right - a - way. _____

ten.

poco rit.

fz

CHORUS.

Well I May Be Cra - zy But I Ain't No Fool; _____
Well I May Be Cra - zy But I Ain't No Fool; _____
Well I May Be Cra - zy But I Ain't No Fool; _____

f *mf*

10,075-3   **WARNING!** Any copying of the words or music of this song, *or any portion thereof,* makes the infringer liable to criminal prosecution under the U. S. Copyright Law....

one and one al - ways makes two___ is___ what I learnt in
I read all 'bout "Buff"- lo Bill" when I was goin' to
three and three al - ways makes six___ is___ what I learnt in

school; 'Cause I have known for___ man - y a year,___ That you
school; There's one thing that's___ a cer - tain - ty,___ He'll___
school; My ri - val said "yes"___ an' grabbed his hat,___ But___

must not b'lieve___ all___ that you hear; Well I May Be
make no tar - - get___ out of me; Well I May Be
I could nev - - er___ love like that; Well I May Be

poco rit. *f* *mf*

1 & 2 *Last time*

Cra - zy, But I Ain't No Fool.___ *D.S.*
Cra - zy, But there was no duel.___
Cra - zy, But I Ain't No fish.___

fz *mp* *D.S.* *fz*

10.075-3

especially the command performances of *In Dahomey* at Buckingham Palace, was a source of pride to many people in Harlem, and newspapers like the New York *Age* implied that every subscriber could be proud to belong to the race that produced Bert Williams and George Walker. Walker made frequent statements to the press, explaining his ambition to elevate his audience. Both he and Williams gave their time generously to benefit performances, but their most important contribution to the advancement of professional standards was the formation of the Frogs, a charitable organization modeled after the American Actors Beneficial Association, from which Negroes had always been barred.

As early as 1905, Williams and Walker, with several other prominent show people—most notably Cole and Johnson, Ernest Hogan, Billy Kersands, and Abbie Mitchell Cook—organized a Colored Actors Beneficial Association, later re-named the Promoters of High Art in Music and Literature, but this club never developed far beyond the planning stage. It wasn't until July, 1908, that a Negro professional organization with any longevity was established. It was named the Frogs, after the characters in Aristophanes' play and Aesop's fable. The founders meant the club's name to symbolize their feelings of dignity and responsi-

THE FROGS

Reading from left to right: Top Row—Bob Cole, Lester A. Walton, Sam Corker, Jr., Bert A. Williams, James Reese Europe, Alex Rogers. Bottom Row—Tom Brown, J. Rosamond Johnson, Geo. W. Walker, J. A. Shipp, R. C. McPherson.

bility. The organization was held in great respect by the Harlem community; as Harrison Smith said, "They were very aristocratic looking gentlemen, all very distinguished. They were a bunch of doers." The Frogs continued for years as a leading professional club, admitting doctors and lawyers as well as theater people to membership.

The Frogs was founded by eleven men: Williams and Walker, Bob Cole, Lester A. Walton, Sam Corker, James Reese Europe, Alex Rogers, Tom Brown, J. Rosamond Johnson, Jesse Shipp, and R.C. McPherson. They first met at Walker's home at 52 West 133rd Street in Harlem and elected him president, with J.R. Johnson vice-president, Jesse Shipp treasurer, Jim Europe librarian, and Bert Williams head of the art committee. The avowed purpose was to form an archive collection for "social, historical, and library purposes" containing all kinds of material for a theatrical library in a clubhouse later built at 111 West 132 Street. The club also raised money for charities.

Probably the most popular function of the Frogs was an annual social event open to the public, a dance and vaudeville revue called the "Frolic of the Frogs" which took place in August. The "Frolic" was for any adult who could afford fifty cents admission. Favors were given to the ladies (the first year it was a green pennant with "F-R-O-G-S" spelled out in white letters), and "three valuable prizes" went to the three people wearing the "most unique and picturesque costume emblematic of the FROGS." The dance usually started at 10:30 and continued all night. The crowds were so large they overflowed the Manhattan Casino, leaving no room for the vaudeville entertainers to perform, so they usually just marched around the hall. The Frolic of the Frogs soon became one of the biggest social events in Harlem.

The popularity of the Frogs was tangible proof that the Harlem community was proud of its members' accomplishments. But George Walker wanted even more recognition. He had a goal for his productions that was unprecedented for Negro shows, for in his time they were lumped into the category of circus attractions in the minds of most white audiences. Since *Sons of Ham,* Walker had been trying to increase the prestige and earning power of the Williams and Walker company so that it could be booked into first class theaters all over the country.

Walker wanted more than the increased box office take that went with the higher admission prices of the better theaters. He felt that the Williams and Walker productions were first class shows and as such reflected on the entire race. If Walker could see his company playing before "the most educated and refined white people in America," he would have achieved his aim—proving that Negroes didn't have to take a back seat to white entertainers, and that "it was possible for the black performer to do better . . . [than] beating the tamborine and rattling the bones." Walker had kept the goal he started with when he left his home in Kansas many years before; he was willing to be as aggressive and forceful as possible, if it meant his dream would be fulfilled.

In one sense Walker had realized part of his ambition. "The Two Real Coons" had played top houses in vaudeville ever since their first appearance in

New York in 1896, and their last three shows had appeared on Broadway. That they had achieved personal success was amply illustrated by the satiric dialogue written by the *Age* reviewer Lester Walton, after overhearing a conversation about Williams and Walker's vaudeville act at the Colonial Theater in 1908:

First young man: *It's a pity these two fellows are colored. I bet if they were white men they would make a barrel of money.*

Second young man: *Yes, they are certainly clever, but I understand they make a very large salary in vaudeville if they are colored.*

First: *Well, I wonder how much they get?*

Second: *I understand about $3,000 a week.*

An Interested Listener: *No, they get $2,000.*

Both young men in unison: *Gee!*

First young man: *That's $1,000 apiece. I don't think that's discriminating on account of color.*

Although it wasn't unusual for single performers to get first class bookings, managers were reluctant to take the risk of placing an entire Negro company in theaters outside New York where admission prices started at $1.50, afraid the show wouldn't attract enough people who could afford the high ticket cost. But before the second year's tour of *Bandana Land,* Walker succeeded in persuading the Shuberts to manage them. In July, 1908, he announced that *Bandana Land* was to play the Savoy Theater in Atlantic City, "considered to be one of the best there," and then the Belasco Theater in Washington, D.C. "This will be the first time a colored show ever played at the Belasco." Walker had finally won the struggle, but he didn't realize his victory would be very short-lived. The coming tour of *Bandana Land* was his last. Within six months, he was forced to leave the company to enter a rest home, suffering from what was at that time an incurable, fatal disease.

Syphilis and its ravaging consequences destroyed many lives before the discovery of penicillin, but the serious nature of the scourge was rarely publicly stressed. When entertainers became infected by the spirochete, the newspapers often treated their illness as a joke, and frequently other actors themselves adopted a callous attitude. In the 1880's, the famous tragedian John McCullough suffered from paresis, the advanced stage of syphilis, but when he insisted upon remaining in the theater despite frequent memory losses and lapses into incoherent frenzy, variety house audiences were regaled with a sordid sketch entitled, "The Ravings of John McCullough." Soon afterwards the popular Tony Hart, of the team of Harrigan and Hart, was the subject of a big black headline in the *New York Herald.*

THAT TELLTALE LISP

*Tony Hart's Trouble Begins Like
That of John McCullough*

All The Symptoms of Paresis

---

*Why Ned Harrigan's Famous Partner
Has Been Forced to Leave the Stage*

Among Negro entertainers the disease took an even larger toll, and there is a depressingly long list of those who succumbed to paresis, among them Ernest Hogan, Bob Cole, Scott Joplin, Louis Chauvin, and George Walker.

Walker's symptoms were the usual sad catalog of memory loss, unpredictable emotional tantrums, unsteady gait, an increasing rough and raspy voice, the suggestion of a lisp, and frequent stuttering. Desperately trying to ignore his growing illness, he managed to continue his role in *Bandana Land* until February 1909, with only occasional times when he was unable to go on. In the summer of 1908, he even danced at a benefit concert for Ernest Hogan, who was in retirement from stage, suffering from the first signs of the paresis that resulted in his death. Soon to be incapacitated himself by this illness, George was such a hit at the concert that one reviewer exclaimed that ". . . in a neat suit, he almost walked in the air."

At Christmas, 1908, Walker wrote a message to the readers of the *Age* titled "Bert and Me and Them," giving a short history of their career and ending with the plea:

> *We want our folks to like us. Not for the sake of the box office, but because over and behind all the money and prestige which move Williams and Walker, is a love for the race. Because we feel that, in a degree, we represent the race and every hair's breadth of achievement we make is to its credit. For first, last, and all the time, we are Negroes. Our payroll is $2300 a week. Figure how many families that's supporting. Williams and Walker are a race institution.*

Continuing bravely despite her husband's sickness, Ada organized a Christmas Cantata in praise of the good fortune and success enjoyed by the Williams and Walker Company, and the composition was sung by the Williams and Walker Literary and Musical Society at their Christmas party. She was depressed and unhappy about her husband's "over-worked nerves," and on the encouragement of friends she began preparations to imitate his theme song in the event of his extended absence. Cartoons of Ada appeared in the newspapers showing her in a straw hat, plaid four-button suit and spats, carrying white gloves and a cane, her bouffant long hair swept under her hat, dressed for her impersonation of the "Bon Bon Buddy."

Walker managed to stay with *Bandana Land* through the first weeks of

1909, but his stuttering was so marked that his performances became increasingly more embarrassing. Finally, unavoidably, the night came when he realized himself that he was through. In the spotlight, strutting bravely before the public, he sang his theme song for the last time.

> *I'm Bon Bon Buddy the Chocolate Drop,*
> *The Chocolate Drop.*
> *I'm Bon Bon Buddy the Chocolate Drop,*
> *The Chocolate Drop that's me.*
> *I've gained no Fame,*
> *But I'm not ashamed,*
> *I'm satisfied with my Nick Name,*
> *I'm Bon Bon Buddy the Chocolate Drop,*
> *The Chocolate Drop that's me.*

Walker wasn't even well enough to see his wife's impersonation of him. He was taken to his home in Lawrence, Kansas, and then confined in a sanitorium in Mt. Clemens, Michigan. A year later he traveled with a "secretary" on a train to New York, hoping that new doctors might be able to cure him, but the paresis had progressed too far. After *Bandana Land,* George Walker never performed in a theater again.

AIDA OVERTON WALKER
IN MALE ATTIRE SINGING "BON BON BUDDY"

I'd Rather Have Nothin' All Of The Time,
Than Somethin' For A Little While.

Words by
JOHN B. LOWITZ.
Swifty.

Music by
BERT A WILLIAMS.

Moderato.

When   I   was   young   I
One   win - t'ry   day   while

al - ways hoped_ that   some   day   I'd   be   rich,_____   I
on   my   way__   to   pawn   my   o - ver - coat,_____   My

got a board the train for wealth_ when some one turned the switch,_ As
ea gle eye it chanced to spy_ a bran new dol-lar note,_ I

soon as I got a-ny-thing 'twas gone be-fore I knew, Just
picked it up and then re-marked, "I will not have to freeze," When

like the foam_ on a glass of beer_ would fly each time I
some one from_ be - hind me said,_ "Re - turn my dol - lar

blew, _____ And as I'd say, "Why how - de - do,"_ and
please," _____ And as I gave that green - back back,_ I

I'd Rather Have Nothin' Etc. 4

think it mine for keeps,____ It al - ways said,_ "Oh
mur - mured, "Good - bye Bill,"____ The best of friends, do

fare thee well," and left in bounds and leaps.____ So I would
sep - a - rate__ this part - ing grieves but still.____ Well I would

Chorus.

rath-er have noth - in' all of the time, than some-thin' for a lit - tle

while, When I have noth - in' I'm not fuss - in' and

I can wear a peace-ful smile,___ When some-thin's leav - in'
then I'm griev - in' noth - in' seems to re - con-cile___
___ So I would rath-er have noth - in' all of the time, than
some-thin' for a lit - tle while. So I would while.___

1.
2.

I'd Rather Have Nothin' Etc. 4

A SHOW IN HIMSELF

BERT WILLIAMS was facing the greatest challenge of his career. Identified in the public's mind as part of a team, he was to go on the stage alone, without Walker, for the first time in more than sixteen years. In 1892 he had been an inexperienced adolescent, and in the subsequent years he had developed a great amount of professional skill, but he had always relied on Walker as a comic foil. He had matured as an artist and received praise for his pantomime and songs, but he worried that appearing alone in a full length musical play was entirely different from delivering a few songs and jokes while his partner was off stage for a few moments.

In early March, 1909, *Bandana Land,* slightly revised for Bert Williams and Ada Overton Walker, opened in Philadelphia. Bert needn't have worried. The verdict of reviewers and general public alike was that Williams was "a show in himself." He had scored a personal success, but after less than a month after reopening he decided not to continue the musical. Unable to replace his partner as business manager, Williams was dismayed trying to guide the large company, and the emotional difficulties of Walker's retirement had exhausted him. In April, 1909, *Bandana Land* played the Yorkville Theater in Brooklyn, the company's last engagement. After the final performance, Williams read aloud to the assembled cast a letter from George Walker that told how much he missed being with the show. Williams added his own comment after he finished the letter: "My one wish is that when the next season opens, my partner will be with me again."

Bert and Lottie Williams had been traveling for over a year, and they welcomed the chance to rest in New York for a few months. They had an apartment on West Ninety-ninth Street, and Williams relaxed among his book collection and exercised on the baseball diamond. New York offered one particular attraction he especially enjoyed, making phonograph records. He recorded for the Columbia Record Company every time he was in the city, and in his recordings from the 1906–1911 period, songs like "Nobody," "He's a Cousin of Mine," "I'll Lend You Anything," and "Constantly," there is a growing assurance to his style and a richer vocal quality.

Williams didn't have to worry about another engagement after *Bandana Land*. He was immediately approached by vaudeville managers, anxious to book him for the late spring season, and it was rumored that he was offered a salary in "four figures." The situation for Negro actors had improved a little in the early years of the twentieth century. The improvement had come largely through the success of Williams and Walker, but other stars and shows, like Cole and Johnson and their new musical *The Red Moon,* and Ernest Hogan and the Black Patti Troubadours, were evidence that Negroes could perform as capably as their white counterparts. By 1909, there were also several shows annually touring theaters in the South, offering vaudeville acts and farces loosely modeled on the Williams and Walker or Cole and Johnson productions. The most successful of these were S. H. Dudley's *His Honor the Barber,* and S. Tutt Whitney's *Southern Smart Set.* On a more refined plane, the William Morris Agency quietly advertised that it was managing the dancing team of Charlie Johnson and Dora Dean.

By the first decade of the twentieth century, serious critics of the drama like James Metcalf had begun to write articles on the possibilities of a Negro theater, saying "The racial problems arising in the new conditions of this country should furnish valuable material to replace the exhausted social perplexities which we have imported from abroad to supply our stage with dramatic situations."

Metcalf was answered by Bob Cole, who wrote eloquently in the New York *Age*,

So with you I shout to the American dramatists, why go to the Rhine or Rome or Greece for your dramatic material? Cast your buckets below! Anywhere you see a Negro there's drama: the dandy darky in the street, the mulatto elevator boy in your fashionable apartment, the Negro criminal in the prison docks. You don't have to go to the "Black Belt" for atmosphere and color. As to your unities—Locale, America; Time, now.

Although performers were slowly becoming more articulate, Bert Williams on the stage never broke from the old idea of what colored actors should be like; he always appeared in blackface. His achievement lay in his artistic method, which communicated a unique warmth and personality behind the caricature. Ever since first putting on the blackface make-up, he had been developing a personal philosophy of comedy, both in theory and in practise on stage, that enabled him to rise above his predicament as a Negro and view his problems in human, not only racial, perspective. He decided that

One of the funniest sights in the world is a man whose hat has been knocked in or ruined by being blown off—provided, of course, it be the other fellow's hat! All the jokes in the world are based on a few elemental ideas, and this is one of them. The sight of other people in trouble is nearly always funny. This is human nature.

Years later, Charlie Chaplin was to ask himself, "What is humor? It is a kind of gentle and benevolent custodian of the mind which prevents us from being overwhelmed by the apparent seriousness of life." Like Chaplin, Bert Williams used his sense of humor to create a stage character who endured and actually triumphed despite the repeated injustices of fate. Williams used his blackface roles to communicate more than the ridiculous quality of the racial stereotype. If the burnt cork mask was his audiences' ideal "coon." he gave it to them, but his stage character went a step further. He was the "Jonah Man," the unluckiest man in the world, resigned to the stupendous weight of his misfortunes through a rueful self-pity that transcended the color bar. Since audiences liked to laugh at the troubles of other people, Bert was the butt of all the jokes, but he never became so foolish that he didn't possess the ultimate dignity of self-preservation. His songs and stories mirrored his concern with a specific theory of comedy.

If you will observe your own conduct whenever you see a friend falling down on the street, you will find that nine times out of ten your first impulse is to laugh and your second is to run and help him get up. To be polite you will dust off his clothes and ask him if he has hurt himself. But when it is all over you cannot resist telling him how funny he looked when he was falling. The man with the real sense of humor is the man who can put himself in the spectator's place and laugh at his own misfortunes.

That is what I am called upon to do every day. Nearly all of my successful songs have been based on the idea that I am getting the worst of it. I am the "Jonah Man," the man who, even if it rained soup, would be found with a fork in his hand and no spoon in sight, the man whose fighting relatives come to visit him and whose head is always dented by the furniture they throw at each other. There are endless variations of this idea, fortunately, but if you sift them, you will find the principle of human nature at the bottom of them all.

Troubles are funny only when you pin them to one particular individual; the fellow who is the goat must be the man who is singing the song or telling the story. Then the audience can picture him in their minds' eye and see him in the thick of his misfortunes, fielding flatirons with his head, carrying large bulldogs by the seat of his pants, and picking the bare bones of the chicken while his wife's relations eat the breast, and so forth.

Williams took his stage role very seriously; he felt that a sense of humor

has to be developed by hard work and study, just as every other human quality. I have studied it all my life, unconsciously during my floundering years and consciously as soon as I began to get next to myself. It is a study that I shall never get to the end of, and a work that never stops.

More than anything else, Williams believed "the entire aim and object of art is to achieve naturalness." He was most interested in *character.*

I try to portray the shiftless darky to the fullest extent; his fun, his philosophy. There is nothing about this fellow I don't know. I must study his movements. I have to. He is not in me. The way he walks; the way he crosses his legs; the way he leans up against a wall, one foot forward. I find much material by knocking around in out of the way places and just listening. Eavesdropping on human nature is one of the most important parts of a comedian's work.

Like all great comedians, Bert Williams was a "particular individual" as well as a comic type on the stage. Over six feet tall, weighing more than two hundred pounds, he possessed a wonderfully inept clumsiness when he moved his big feet or body, and long graceful hands that expressed paragraphs with a gesture's economy. His voice was deep and low, with an "unction" or smoothness of Southern dialect and inflection born of long hours of practise and experiment. He delivered his lines very slowly and deliberately, as though from the recesses of some dimly private self-regard. When he sang it was with an inimitable syncopation—rhythmic slurs, pauses and off-beats that kept his songs freshly individual. He was able to suggest a human presence behind the blackface, even if his humor was usually confined to racial material.

Developing strength as a "single" performer, Williams experimented in vaudeville during the summer of 1909 with a new group of dialect stories which he called "lies," jokes which had a flavor of folklore and fable. Alex Rogers made a collection of the "lies," writing them down for Williams in a copybook. The one about the circus lion was a favorite.

One time I was stranded in a town an' a circus come along, so I went an' told the manager that I was desperate an' jus' had to have work. He said, "Well, one of our best lions died last week and as we saved the skin, if you want to you can git in it and be a lion till somethin' better comes along."

Naturally I grabbed it and that same afternoon I made my first 'pearance as "The King of the Jungles." Then here comes the man what does the stunts inside of the animals' cages. He come in my cage first an' after 'splainin' 'bout what a fine specimen I was and how much trouble they had ketchin' me in Africa, he say,

"Now ladies and gen'men to show you how much we have tamed and trained him, I am goin' to turn him into this next cage with this large and f'rocious Bengal Tagger."

I imeegitly backed into the furthest corner of my cage. The man opened up the door between the two cages, drawed out a big pistol an' say, "Git in there or I'll blow yo' head off." An' kinder under his breath he say to me, "And that goes, too."

And then he took and fired the gun off once up over his head to show me that it would shoot and I looked up and seen the hole it made in the roof of the cage so I jus' went on in the next cage and got right down on my knees and commence prayin'. And this big Bengal tagger leaped toward me and jus' as my heart was gettin' ready to stop for good, that tagger took and leaned over and I heard him whisper right in my ear, "Don't be skeered, pal. I'm colored same as you."

In his past shows, *Abyssinia* and *Bandana Land,* Williams had been given increasing opportunity to show his skill in pantomime. In *Bandana Land* he had introduced a song, "Late Hours," which preceded his most famous pantomime, the poker game skit. He performed it over and over in vaudeville, and even filmed it in a silent movie made in 1914. With no props other than a table and chair, he was able to suggest, with subtle changes of facial expression, what cards each of five players was holding, how the bets were made, and who won the pot. Tom Fletcher gave the source of the famous poker game.

Bert himself told me, one night in the back room of Matheney's Cafe on 125th Street and Seventh Avenue, where he got the idea for his pantomime poker game. He said it was while playing in Lincoln, Nebraska, he went to see an old friend in a hospital. The guard said to him, "Would you like to walk around with me and see the place?" He accepted the invitation and the guard first took him to see the patients that were almost ready to leave the hospital. Then the guard took him to another part of the hospital where the patients were very

106

ill. There was one fellow in a room, alone. Evidently his mental illness was due to gambling, playing poker. In his room was a table and a chair. He was there all alone, talking to himself and acting as though he were in a poker game for he would go through the motions of having a drink, looking around the table and smiling at the other players. He would reach in his imaginary pile of chips and throw in his ante, looking around to see if everybody was in, then smile again. He would shuffle and begin to deal around and after he finished dealing, he would pick up his imaginary hand and look at each player after they had discarded, to see how many cards they wanted. All this time he would have a smile on his face as if he believed he had the best hand, and as each player asked for cards his smile would get broader. As each imaginary player would ask for cards he would put up fingers to show he understood how many. Then, when one of the imaginary players stood pat, his smile would suddenly begin to vanish. When the deal was all over, the betting would start. Each player would call or pass. When it was up to him he would look at his hand, put it down, pour a little drink from his imaginary bottle and look again. Then he would push in the last of his chips and call.

After the showdown he had the second best hand. He would stand up, brush off his pants and go back to his bunk, place his elbows on his knees and leaning on his hands, shake his head slowly.

Bert stood there and watched the man. Jesse Shipp, who was with Williams, broke the silence and said, "Bert, there you are."

The poker game skit became famous, but Williams was best known for a song, "Nobody." He started singing it in vaudeville during the summer of 1905, thinking of it as just another song of the "Jonah Man" type. To his surprise, the audiences response threatened to get out of hand. Williams once said,

Before I got through with "Nobody" I could have wished that both the author of the words and the assembler of the tune had been strangled or drowned or talked to death. For seven whole years I had to sing it. Month after month I tried to drop it and sing something new, but I could get nothing to replace it and the audiences seemed to want nothing else.

To spark some enthusiasm in himself for his endless repetitions, Bert worked the song into a regular act. He pretended he found it difficult to remember Jesse Shipp's words, and he began to read them off a piece of paper, deliberately pulling a little notebook from his pocket and hesitatingly finding the right page, before half-singing, half-reciting the song. He couldn't win. Audiences loved "Nobody" even more for his reluctance and delay.

In late summer of 1909, after two months of vaudeville appearances in Boston, New York, Pittsburgh, Philadelphia, Detroit, Buffalo, and Rockaway Beach, Williams decided to try to carry on the traditional Williams and Walker full length, all-Negro production with himself as star. Jesse Shipp and Alex Rogers started on the book and lyrics, J. Rosamund Johnson began composing the musical numbers, and many of the performers in the old Williams and Walker company gathered for rehearsals. The only serious drawback to Bert's plans was that Ada Overton Walker declined signing with the new show. The *Age* reported that she had been offered a contract, but "she and the management have not been able to agree on several items." Finally when Ada took over the lead actress's role in Cole and Johnson's *The Red Moon,* Williams signed a young showgirl, Lottie Grady, from the Pekin Theater in Chicago, to play opposite him.

The new show, *Mr. Lode of Koal,* was a slight fantasy with the action centering around Mr. Lode's (played by Williams) dream that he had been shipwrecked on an island where all the natives were deluded into a belief that someday their real ruler would be sent to them from the sea. When Williams was washed ashore on this island, the natives proclaimed him king. Unhappy about being a monarch, he tried to escape, but he was surrounded by so many vigilant bodyguards that it seemed he must remain king forever. Bert's many futile attempts to forsake his throne and leave the island were the basis for the comedy.

Critics enjoyed his acting and gave mild praise to his new songs, which weren't outstanding: "My Old Man," "The Christening," and "That's A Plenty." After only six months on the road touring in second rate theaters, *Mr. Lode of Koal* gave its last performance on March 5, 1910, at the Court Street Theater in Brooklyn. Williams went back to vaudeville.

As a celebrity he played the best theaters in Boston and Philadelphia during the early spring, and he appeared happy to be free of the obligations of maintaining his own company. As a single performer in a white man's world Bert expected to meet hostility in his professional life, but nevertheless he tried to be as cooperative as possible. In vaudeville with white performers, he could play the top houses, but he could never headline the bill. Instead Bert Williams' name was set in second place, although in the largest, darkest type on the program. Even donating his services to benefit performances, he faced constant slights. When he was asked to appear at an annual Friar's Frolic charity benefit, he accepted, although he wasn't a Friar (Negroes couldn't belong to the organization). Arriving at the New York Theater, he found that there were more stars than dressing rooms, and the stage manager asked the men to double up, more than one to a room. Williams stood looking about him, and as the others paired off, he slowly moved back toward the street door. If none of the Friars wanted to dress with him, he was going home. Near the threshold he stood still, waiting. The door opened after a few moments and George Cohan walked in. He took a glance around the stage and spying Williams in the corner, Cohan grasped the situation immediately. He went up to him and shook his hand warmly. "Thank you for coming to help us out with the Frolic tonight," he told Williams; "come on, Bert, you're dressing with me."

Williams knew he faced hostility wherever he went, for like the character Mr. Lode of Koal, he couldn't leave a desert island—the predicament of being a Negro in America. Incidents like the Friar's benefit only confirmed his hope that if he didn't push himself on people, his skill as an entertainer would bear mute testimony to his worth as a human being. He didn't try to disguise his identification with the Negro people, however. Two weeks after the Friar's benefit, he accepted his election as President of the Frogs. But he debated endlessly with himself the best course to follow in his career. As the top ranking comedian in the United States, he could do anything he wished—stay in America or return to England, where he had found less flagrant social humiliation. He could organize his own company again, stay in vaudeville as a single, or he could accept a very challenging offer that had recently been suggested to him. He decided to try something new, and in May, 1910, newspapers announced that Bert Williams would be a feature in Florenz Ziegfeld's Follies of 1910.

He's A Cousin Of Mine

Words by
Cecil Mack

Music by
Chris. Smith &
Silvio Hein

1. There's a scan-dal in the
2. When she had ex-plained her

neigh-bor-hood__ And it's all 'bout Jul-ie Brown_____ It
re-la-tion-ship__ He re-plied "It may be so"_____ But

seems her long lost cou - sin, Jer - e - mi - ah, Had late - ly ar - rived in
he don't look like a thir - ty-sec-ond cou-sin That I met a week a-

town _____ When Jul - ie's "fel - ler" came to call that
go _____ She smiled at him quite in - no-cent-ly ____ and

Sun - day at her home, _____ He found the pair a-
blushed up to her hair, _____ Then said, "If you don't

sit - ting there Jes' a spoon - ing in the gloam, _____ The
want him 'round I will tell him so, my dear, _____ She

poco rit.

sight made him so riled _____ he start-ed home at once _____ But
joined her cou-sin's side _____ and as they stroll'd a - way _____ He

rit.

Jul - ie said "I'm s'prised at you, don't go act like a dunce:" _____
heard him ask "Who is that freak" and heard his Jul - ie say: _____

rit.

sfz

Chorus

Why He's A Cou-sin Of Mine,— Just a cou-sin of mine,— You're

p-f

li' - ble for to see him here an - y old time,—

Jes' like a bee you're all the time a buzz-in' 'Taint no harm for to hug and kiss your cou-sin, I have-n't seen Jer-ry, in the last ten years, You know that's a might-y long time_____ He's moth-er's sis - ter's an - gel child, (SPOKEN) (G'wan man) He's A Cou-sin Of Mine."_ Why He's A

THE FOLLIES

In this day and time when it appears that from certain quarters an effort is being made to hide the light of the colored performer under a bushel—in fact, a peck or quart measure would describe conditions more fittingly—it affords one much pleasure to note that there is one colored light which refused to be covered up or put in eclipse; and that is Bert Williams.

Monday evening, Ziegfeld's FOLLIES OF 1910 was seen in New York City for the first time on the New York Theater roof. The show is on an elaborate scale, two acts and thirteen scenes, yet in this pretentious musical review, the work of the colored comedian stands boldly out, from an artistic standpoint, above everybody and everything.

At the bottom of the program appears inconspicuously the name of Mr. Williams, in which he is defined as being known as "The Caretaker" in the cast. . . . [but] All the critics refer to Bert Williams as the feature of the FOLLIES OF 1910.

The New York *Age,* June 23, 1910

BERT WILLIAMS was recognized as "the feature" in his first years with the Ziegfeld shows, when his talent reached thousands of people who had come to the Follies for a look at the chorus girls and top name entertainers. In the midst of Ziegfeld's lavish sets and vivacious women, the work of the tall, slow moving man in blackface stood out brilliantly.

Ziegfeld had been producing his reviews since 1907, when he starred his wife, the French singer Anna Held, in a musical extravaganza in which she led a group of young chorus girls in songs and dances. Miss Held incorporated her knowledge of the Paris music halls into Ziegfeld's shows, contributing the happy idea of scantily dressed models in flesh colored tights posed on stage amid veils and flowers. As the Follies box office flourished, Ziegfeld was able to attract bigger vaudeville names, until in only a few years after his first Follies he was starring the best music hall artists.

The Follies of 1910 cost fifty thousand dollars and presented more than sixty starlets during the evening's entertainment. Bert Williams, always sensitive to the slightest possibility of racial protest, insisted that his contract with Ziegfeld included a clause "that at no time would he be on stage with any of the female members of the company." Ziegfeld agreed, realizing that some people in his audience would object strongly to a Negro showman "mixing" with white women. But in return, Ziegfeld promised that the Follies would never include Southern cities in its annual tours; this was promised as a favor to Williams, who Ziegfeld knew never appeared below the Mason-Dixon line.

The Follies of 1910 opened in June in its usual home in the Jardin de Paris, an enclosed "summer and winter garden" on top of the New York Theater. Besides the "60—Anna Held Girls—60," the cast included such stars as Anna Held, Lillian Lorraine, Fannie Brice, Julian Mitchell, Bobby North, Harry Watson, Grace Tyler, Louise Alexander, and Billy Reeves. Bickel and Watson's Roosevelt Band were included in the advertised "Cast of 125."

With words by Harry B. Smith and music by Gus Edwards "and many others," the "Song Revue Follies of 1910" continued Ziegfeld's three-year-old formula of visual beauty incidently interrupted by skits and songs. Williams was billed as "The Blackbird with Songs," and he sang and acted so impressively that he was given top praise. The Chicago *Evening American* reviewer felt,

> *It is quite interesting as well as instructive to contrast his methods with those of some of Mr. Ziegfeld's other entertainers, to see Williams produce surely his intended effect by art, by deft suggestion, and mental projection crystalized by a tone, a look, a gesture, or merely a pause—and to see others turn three somersaults, repeat the joke for times, then blow it through a trombone, wave two flags over it and fall downstairs with seven tons of glass and then "not get over."*

And Ashton Stevens wrote in the Chicago *Examiner:* "Bert Williams is the Mark Twain of his color. . . . His was kindly, infectious humor, humor that made humans of us all."

Williams' prestige had greatly increased with his affiliation with the Follies, but when the show finished its tour in San Francisco in May, 1911, he returned to New York City and continued to live simply with Lottie in their apartment on Ninety-ninth Street. He found the work with the Follies less demanding in some ways; no longer the star in his own show, he was not pressed with the details and constant responsibilities of a large company. Williams had freed himself of production worries and had only to concentrate on his skits and songs. He got along well with Ziegfeld, staying clear of most of the other members of the Follies, always careful to retain his dignity and self-respect if challenged. His main social contact was with the men in the chorus, who asked if he'd like to be captain of their baseball team, which met on Sundays to play the stagehands. Bert accepted, playing first base. Tom Fletcher remembered that at this time he started having trouble with his feet. They swelled painfully, and Williams took extra special care not to injure them. He was dancing a little in his Follies act, in one skit wearing a rooster's costume to make an awkward entrance on stage out of a large papier-mache egg, but he tried to take as good care of his feet as possible. The baseball players on the opposing teams took great advantage of his difficulty. Whenever a batter began charging down the line to first base, he would immediately switch from making a possible put-out to protecting his feet, and often he would stay far away from the bag regardless of whether or not he had a chance to put the runner out.

Williams' swelling feet were an early indication of poor circulation and a weakening heart, but he was still an active man. However, on January 6, 1911, with the Follies still playing New York City before leaving for the West, George Walker died. Walker had left the Michigan sanitorium six months before to enter the New York state mental hospital at Central Islip, Long Island, where he was receiving the best possible medical treatment for what was already a hopelessly advanced case of syphilis. Williams had given up any thought of Walker's recovering to the point of reestablishing the partnership, but the death was a shock to him. He paid the expenses of Walker's long medical treatment, as well as the charges for shipping Walker's body to Lawrence, Kansas, for burial. In a statement to the *Age,* Williams said that the theatrical profession had lost a most significant performer, who had as his chief aim "to elevate the colored theatrical profession and the race as well."

The Late George Walker

Familiar Poses of the Late George Walker

In the two years since Walker's forced retirement, Williams had come to see that there were advantages to working alone. Walker had insisted on productions that emphasized what he called "African" elements, like *In Dahomey* and *Abyssinia.* In *Mr. Lode of Koal* and the Follies, Williams tried to remove himself a little further from a strong racial emphasis so that his characterizations could be seen in a wider variety of situations. With slightly more latitude, he sometimes transcended the blackface sterotype completely, as in songs like "My Landlady."

My ma and pa always taught me never to ignore nobody.
But there's one person that I hate to see,
That's my landlady.
Umm, she knows exactly when you owe,
She don't need no almanac to show,
She don't even care about your funds bein' low,
That is—my landlady.

(Chorus)
But just like a ghost through the halls she's always sneakin',
You owe your rent, round your door she starts sweepin',
You in the room crazy, holdin' your head, and thinkin'
What excuse can I give my landlady?
She seems to know exactly when yo' tellin' a lie,
If there's one female I do despise,
It's my landlady.

Flirtin' on the street 'tother day on the q.t. Ha ha!
I met a gal that looked like she was over a block from me.
And when I got close enought to see,
It turned out to be my landlady.
If the law would only allow me to have full sway with the third degree,
The first person I'd put through it would be my landlady.

(Chorus)
But just like a ghost through the halls she's always sneakin',
You owe your rent, round your door she starts sweepin',
You in the room crazy, holdin' your head, and thinkin'
What excuse can I give my landlady?
She never has got any vaudeville "lieber,"
She's the champion transom and keyhole peeper,
Who goes through your trunk like a vacuum sweeper?
Huh—my landlady.

In this song Williams was any down-and-out lodger who dreaded his landlady, and his human frailty—"Flirtin' on the street 'tother day on the q.t."—was genuinely comical. The pauses, clearings of the throat, hums, and grimaces that he added during his delivery of the song were accomplished acting, and the 1913 phonograph record of "My Landlady" was a classic of its type. In the Follies, Williams could sing and act in dramatic sketches that brought him beyond the limitations of the supposed "native African elements" Walker was so enthusiastic about exploiting.

Williams' songs and skits in the Follies of 1911 were very successful. Unlike the previous year, when he had not been able to get much good material, he now had the clever "Woodman, Spare That Tree (The Only One My Wife Can't Climb)" and "That's Harmony," which he used to introduce his poker game pantomime. But it was the memorable comic sketch that he did with Leon Errol which caused the reviewer for the New York *Evening Mail* to cry, "Bert Williams makes the need of a White Hope on the Jardin de Paris stage as imperative as Jack Johnson did in the squared ring."

In the sketch, Williams acted the part of a porter who was trying to help Leon Errol, a British tourist, catch a train to New Rochelle. They were forced to ascend to the upper level of Grand Central station, a long and hazardous trip because the entire place was torn up and filled with temporary passages, exposed girders, and unfinished iron work, all signs of the subway construction current in New York City in 1911.

Errol was small and slight, a decided contrast to Williams' height and build. He was also a "fidgety comedian," making so many abrupt, nervous motions that Williams, as the Red Cap, tied a rope to him as a safety measure and wound the other end around his own waist. They proceeded cautiously along the girders like mountain climbers in the Swiss Alps, when suddenly Errol became impressed with the structural work and stopped in the center of the stage to discuss it. Williams had seen plenty already, and he expressed no reaction to Errol's enthusiasm except a fear that the tourist might fall. Errol's nervous little movements and wide gestures finally were a little too much, and he fell off a girder plainly marked "160 Foot Drop." Williams pulled him back with a labored hand-over-hand pull, but just as he succeeded in getting the struggling man to a foothold, Errol asked him, "Porter, have you a match?"

With an exceedingly single-track mind, Williams immediately let go of the rope to search in his pockets for a match. Realizing the Britisher was falling again, he quickly pulled the rope and hauled Errol once more back to the girder. Williams was gasping for breath at this point, but as Errol caught hold of the girder he managed to say, "Never mind the match, Porter, I broke my pipe."

Standing together once more, the two comedians had a fifteen minute exchange of dialogue, Errol asking Williams many questions about the terminal, and about the colored man's work and home life.

"You have a wife and family, I suppose?"
"Oh yes sir; I's married an I'se got three chil'un."
"Is that so. Ah, that's very commendable."
"Yes sir, so it is."
"What are the names of your children?"
"Well, I names 'em out de Bible. Dar's Hannah and den dar's Samuel and de las' I name 'Iwilla'."
"Iwilla? I don't remember that name in the Bible."
"Sure 'tis. Don't you 'member where it say, IWILLA RISE?"

The two men climbed higher on the girders in their search for the train to New Rochelle. Finally they sat down to rest. Williams casually pulled out a lunch pail, explaining that his wife always sent him to work with a good meal—ham and biscuits today. He described the lunch he was going to have so enthusiastically that Errol turned curiously to see it, and carelessly knocked the lunch pail off the girder. It fell a hundred feet, irretrievably lost. Williams just nodded his head, tapping his fingers on his knees, looking at Errol.

To make amends, Errol promised him a good tip—five cents. When he gave Williams the nickel, the porter took it with marked scorn. Suddenly Errol slipped again, this time down the side of a girder marked "288 Foot Drop." The coil of rope around Williams' waist jerked as if Errol would never reach bottom, but the porter only stared deadpan into the laughter of the audience, bracing himself as best he could, then flinching against the tug of the rope that indicated Errol had fallen several stories into the excavation pit.

Williams muttered, "Five cents!", determinedly untied the knot of the rope at his waist, and watched it whiz down the side of the girder. Then he picked up the suitcase he'd been carrying for the tourist and hurled it after him. There was a terrific explosion at this point—the workmen below were blasting rock—while Williams looked off into space and said, "There he goes, way up!", as if the dynamite blast had thrown Errol high in the air. Williams continued, "Ah, there he goes, now he's near the Metropolitan Tower. Ef he kin only grab that little gold ball on the top—um, he muffed it!"

The following year, Williams and Errol were also paired in the best comedy routine of the Follies of 1912, the famous sketch involving the drunk and the antiquated cab. The curtains opened to reveal the oldest living horse in New York City, "Nicodemus," an equally battered cab, and a shabby driver, Bert Williams, stationed in front of a set painted to resemble a view of Seventh Avenue at Forty-seventh Street. Williams was dusting his cab and polishing the head-lamps in desultory fashion, while the patient horse (played by two acrobats inside a drab white horse skin) crossed and uncrossed his legs, looking as if at any moment he might collapse entirely. Every time the horse swayed with its own fatigue and infirmity, Williams solemnly commanded "whoa."

After a short time, Leon Errol wandered onstage, immaculately dressed in evening clothes, a smart overcoat, and an opera hat. Recognizing that the fare was very drunk, Williams decided to cheat him.

> *"Where do you want to go, boss?"*
> *"I wanna go sebalabaloo."*
> *"Oh, you want to go to Seventh Avenue?"*
> *"Yesh, I wanna go sebalabaloo. Y'know wher 'tis?"*

Williams looked him over carefully and made sure no one heard before he replied, "Oh yes, I know where 'tis. Git in an' I'll drive you dar. I know where 'tis all right. It's fur!"

The audience knew from the street sign painted on the backdrop that they were already on Seventh Avenue, and that Williams was going to drive his drunken fare all around the city, bringing him back to the spot where they started. However, when the old horse heard his master say that the distance was far, he started to shake as if he were about to drop from exhaustion. Williams ran up to him quickly, whispering in his ear, "Oats, Nicodemus, OATS." Reassured, the horse straightened up, trying to look alert.

Errol began to climb into the cab, but he was unable to manage the steps until he took a lamp from the socket by the door and proceeded as if going upstairs in his own home. Drunkenly, he wished Williams goodnight. The curtains of the cab were drawn, and Nicodemus slowly wheeled it away.

Williams enjoyed working with Leon Errol in the Follies of 1911 and 1912, and later Errol recalled his pleasure in their association.

Bert Williams and I got along famously. He was the most companionable of men and his keen intelligence, with its underlying vein of genuine humor, was ever a delight and often a surprise.

Of course, the general public has an idea that these funny sketches in which Williams and I were featured from time to time in the Follies, had been furnished us in manuscript by some prominent playwright and that all we had to do, to be funny, was to follow the scenes and lines laid down. Such, however, is far from the truth.

In fact we never knew, before rehearsals began, just what form our portion of the entertainment was to take. About all the authors ever did, in all of the long series in which we appeared, was to indicate in a certain point in the manuscript—probably following a spectacular, sartorial number done by a bevy of beauties, that there was to follow a "comedy number by Errol and Williams."

Our method of procedure thereafter was for Bert and myself to go off into some dim quiet corner of the auditorium or to a vacant dressing room, first decide upon the character in a general way and then, after suggestion and counter suggestion, innumerable as to incidents, gradually each suggest a line of dialog or a quip. He would make notes and lo and behold, we would have the framework of the sketch.

But more than this was necessary. The most important part was yet to come and that was the placing of the "laughs" where they would be most effective. This could only be worked out by continual rehearsals in private. Even the manager knew little or nothing, except in a very general way, of the miniature comedy until it was first shown at a dress rehearsal.

Bert Williams was always most resourceful. The public probably remembers some of the old skits; for instance, the one . . . in which he played a colored cab driver and I the "souse" fare.

Bert Williams was delighted when, after a search of several days, we found an antiquated, dilapidated cab reposing in the storage yard of a West Side dealer in such antiques. We set about damaging it almost beyond recognition and daubing it with paint, to give a more decrepit and a more traveled appearance to it.

120

Bert and I hired a horse to drag the disreputable looking hack down to the theater, with ourselves enthroned within, all apparently oblivious to the hoots and derisive shouts of the multitude. We stood it, until within a block of the theater, when Williams, his sense of humor ever alert, suggested we get out, release the horse and driver, and ourselves draw the chariot to the stage door. No sooner said than done. We paid the man off and each grasping a shaky shaft, started on a run for the stage door, two hundred feet away.

As we neared the theater I realized that the great double scenery doors were wide open and as we ran I shouted to Bert, "Right in on the stage!" He got me instantly, and the way we wheeled from the roadway, across the sidewalk and right in onto the stage in the midst of a hundred rehearsing men and women, was a flourish in tour de force that would have done credit to the chariot racers in "Ben Hur," and it created almost as much excitement as that celebrated scene when we tore in and temporarily broke up the rehearsal. It was too much for the risibilities of Williams. He just lay down on the floor and rolled about in ecstatic joy.

With longer comic scenes every year in Ziegfeld's show, Williams seemed to have found the best place for his performances. But he felt there were difficulties. It was no secret that he was constantly in search of good humorous material, jokes and songs for his act. Nevertheless, it came as a surprise to most of his fans when he announced that he would not appear with the Follies of 1913.

Ziegfeld Follies
Annual Revue

The
Tango
Lesson

Leon Errol

MAKING GOOD
IN THE SUPERLATIVE DEGREE

HARRISON SMITH echoed the thoughts of most New York entertainers when he said, "The fact you worked for Ziegfeld, you were on top of the world." But Williams had had three years in the Follies, and although he was one of the most effective stars in the show, he decided he had had enough of the review for awhile. Instead of signing another three year contract with Erlanger and Ziegfeld, he rested in New York City.

He had become interested in a house that was for sale in Harlem at 2309 Seventh Avenue, near 135th Street. His parents had come from California to live with him and Lottie, and the apartment on Ninety-ninth Street was crowded, so Williams bought the house on Seventh Avenue, a four-story brownstone, the seventh house from the corner in a block filled with adjoining newly built homes of similar design. It was a pleasant neighborhood. The block of houses all faced a narrow strip of trees that extended down Seventh Avenue, and in the rear, each building opened onto a small enclosed garden. At the present time three different people inhabit Williams' house: a lady who lives on the top floors, a lawyer who has offices on the first floor, and a real estate broker whose sign is painted on the wide basement window, below the sidewalk level. But forty-five years ago, when Williams owned the house, Lottie supervised its elaborate decoration, installing marble entrance steps, marble paneling, and carved tiles in the hallway. She arranged many built-in bookcases throughout the house to accommodate her husband's extensive book collection. The pleasant, large back parlor had tall windows looking out into the courtyard garden, with flowers and trees spaced carefully between patterns of inlaid bricks. Williams liked to sit in this parlor and read, but often after the theater, insomnia made him restless. Then he would leave his books and, still in his carpet slippers, walk across the street, past the small park of grass and trees along the middle of Seventh Avenue, to Matheney's Cafe at the corner of 135th Street, where he stayed until dawn.

He had been drinking heavily for years, never causing any disturbance or scandal, and he always tried to have friends with him. One entertainer remembers being with him at Tom Smith's club in Baltimore in 1912, when Williams was touring with the Follies. After the evening's performance, the comedian spent the night at Tom Smith's, playing the piano and singing with Eubie Blake and Noble Sissle, two young song writers appearing in a vaudeville show in that city.

Regardless of how much he had drunk, Williams never lost his self-control, but sometimes this was not enough to appease his wife. Eubie Blake remembers meeting him unexpectedly at dawn when he was just coming out of Matheney's. Williams was very drunk and affectionately put his arm around Blake. "Come home with me," Bert begged, "and help me meet Lottie." Somewhere during the night he had picked up a loaf of bread, "a present for mother," he explained, but Blake went along very reluctantly; Lottie Williams was well known for the strict watch she kept over her husband. As the two men walked up the marble steps of Williams' home, a window curtain twitched suspiciously. The door flew open and Lottie was before them, standing with her hands on her hips. "What have you done to my husband?" she asked Blake accusingly. Williams paused on the steps. "Now mother," he began, and motioned for Blake to take off. Eubie didn't need a second invitation.

During the summer of 1913, the Frogs organization began making plans for its traditional August Frolic, and Williams, who was president of the club, thought it might be a pleasant novelty to stage a big variety entertainment. The rest of the Club were more than willing, and the newspapers announced that for the first time in several years, Williams was going to perform in an all-Negro show.

The Frogs also asked Ada Overton Walker, who was then touring with S.H. Dudley's *Smart Set* company, to join them. This was one of her last appearances in the theater; she was suffering from a kidney infection and soon after her Frogs performance she retired from the stage. S.H. Dudley also acted in a comical skit with Bert Williams, where Dudley was an old "gentleman friend" and Williams a "dusky damsel." Bert had never impersonated a woman before, but in this role he cavorted in a tight slit skirt and a feather boa. The Frogs were using the music of an "exclusive society orchestra" under the direction of James Reese Europe to add further appeal. Europe's orchestra accompanied almost all of the numbers; the first part of the two hour show was organized as a minstrel production, the second half as a vaudeville olio.

The Frogs' show was so successful in its one performance at the Manhattan Casino on August 11th, that a week's tour was arranged to four large cities in the east—Philadelphia, Baltimore, Richmond, and Washington, D.C. The company traveled by train, with the theater managers in the various cities (except Richmond) promising that segregation of patrons in the audience would not be permitted. Williams had never played so far south as Richmond, and he was apprehensive about this performance, but it was in Baltimore that the only racial disturbance occurred; the advertisement for the Frogs' show in the Baltimore newspaper had mentioned that special sections of the theater would be reserved to seat white people, and crowds of Negroes protested and boycotted the theater. In Richmond, advance ticket sales were so large that the original plan to book the show at the Hypodrome Theater was changed so that the performance took place in the city auditorium. Three thousand people were seated in the audience, and hundreds more stood. Because of the crowds, several traditions were broken. In addition to helping the white attendants sell tickets at the box office, Negroes also collected tickets at the door. When the segregated section for whites became overcrowded, they sat with the Negroes. The Richmond *Times-Dispatch* commented that the "audience, although packed, behaved with perfect decorum" to see the Frogs, "the ultimate in ragtime singing and dancing."

After touring with the Frogs, Williams decided not to establish another company of his own. It wasn't that the show hadn't been a success—the entire cast had been warmly entertained with parades, tours, dinners, and midnight dances in their honor given by leading Negro social organizations in each of the cities. It was also not the expense of organizing his own company, since Williams probably could have gotten sufficient financial backing. But rather, the reason was that with the tragic deaths of George Walker, Ernest Hogan, and Bob Cole, there were not any sufficiently prominent stage personalities to join with him in a first-class musical play. S.H. Dudley, who had the biggest name in the touring shows, wished to remain with his own company, and Williams felt he needed another strong performer and manager like Walker to help make his productions function smoothly. Instead, in the fall of 1914, before the rehearsals for the Follies began, Williams signed to appear for a season in vaudeville with the Keith Circuit for two thousand dollars a week. After his success with Ziegfeld, Williams' name had sufficient prestige not only for the large salary, but also—for the first time in his career—for headline billing.

Williams had ample evidence that Negro performers had not achieved wide recognition on stage. He was the only entertainer with sufficient prestige to play first-class Keith theaters on the vaudeville circuit; even performers so successful as S.H. Dudley and Ada Overton Walker appeared primarily before segregated audiences in second rate theaters. There was also a considerable amount of "jim crow" tactics strong on Broadway. When the Shubert's colossal production *America* opened at the New York Hippodrome theater, it was advertised as a panorama of American life and people. But while authentic Indians were brought in from the West, no Negroes appeared in the show. White actors in blackface portrayed porters and redcaps, and the New Orleans levee scene featured blacked-up white men.

Williams and Walker had done a little to break down the traditional barriers, but progress was very slow. Although individual performers could choose whether or not to conform to the stereotypes in vaudeville, these stereotypes were the rule, rather than the exception. What Williams had achieved of importance was showing that on the stage there was a human being behind the blackface caricature. In his private life he had also demonstrated that a Negro could have personal dignity. Despite his great reputation, a misinterpreted gesture, an impatient phrase, even a hint of impropriety in his personal life would have been enough to end his career. Williams walked a tight rope all his life, but his reputation was a good evidence against the arguments of bigots who believed in innate racial inferiority.

Along with Williams' personal success, another factor was operating in popular entertainment at this time that was destined to bring further recognition to Negro talent: the beginning of the "Jazz Age." Syncopated music had been popular in the "raggy motion" of songs and piano music since the beginning of the century, but it wasn't until 1911, when Harlem instrumentalists were organized by James Reese Europe into the Clef Club, that the orchestras really got a chance to be heard. Like the cakewalk craze that had made Williams and Walker popular more than fifteen years before, the new enthusiasm for jazz carried with it a new recognition for the Negro. The jazz orchestras brought wide attention to the skill of instrumentalists, just as the singers, dancers and comedians had been praised before in the Williams and Walker, Black Patti, Ernest Hogan, and Cole and Johnson shows.

Clef Club orchestras were hired for society parties and dances, and by January, 1914, when Williams opened at the Palace with headline honors, Hammerstein's Victoria Theater had James Reese Europe conducting a pit orchestra for Vernon and Irene Castle, popularizers of new dance steps like the fox trot. The rhythm and exuberance of the orchestra was such an attraction that it was later moved to the stage of the theater, the first time a Negro orchestra had ever played in a first-class theater. Dressed in formal clothes, Jim Europe and his orchestra performed with great skill and accomplishment. They were no longer restricted to eccentric, shabby costumes and the jangling banjo, tamborine and bones of the minstrel stage.

Bert Williams found the Follies had changed somewhat during his absence. Ziegfeld's revue had moved to the New Amsterdam Theater, a much more luxurious setting than the old Jardin de Paris. The lobby of the New Amsterdam was richly paneled with murals featuring elegant peacocks, and just above the winding staircase of the spacious entrance hall were large framed displays of the photographs of Follies girls, giving "the effect of a gallery of the more illustrious graduates of some rather smart college," as Edmund Wilson later described it. Along with this new refinement, ticket prices to the Follies rose accordingly, until street barkers sold front seat tickets for $5 before each performance. Rejoining Ziegfeld's show in 1914, Williams stayed with "the luxury . . . and the rich haze of the New Amsterdam" until 1918.

The new theater reflected the fact that Ziegfeld had added a slicker, faster pace to his show. More chorus girls, singers, and dancers were hired, as well as a number of very gifted young comedians. Williams no longer found himself the mainstay of the show's humor. In the Follies of 1914, W.C. Fields, as well as Ed Wynn, were performing. Will Rogers joined the Follies in 1916, Eddie Cantor in 1917. Williams' ability to amuse audiences didn't diminish, but with major talent like Wynn, Fields, Rogers, and Cantor also in the Follies, less time was available for Williams' skits and songs. Also, unfortunately, his material was frequently poor; again he encountered his previous trouble finding writers with genuinely funny ideas. He was frequently reduced to delivering such trite and topical numbers as one of his songs from the 1914 Follies, "The Man That Wrote 'The Vampire' Must Have Known My Wife."

Williams had a few high points during the Follies of 1914–1917, however. In 1915 he was in a sophisticated sketch written by Gene Buck, satirizing the inhabitants of a fashionable New York apartment house. The *New York Times* reviewer liked it very much: "The dialogue is brilliant and the sketch of such apartment life as it is, strikingly true." Bert played the switchboard attendant on duty in the apartment lobby around 1 a.m. The tenants (mostly women) and the callers (mostly men) went in and out when they were not overworking Williams on the phone. He knew them all, the kind of people who "may be found all over the West Side of Manhattan between 42nd and 135th Streets." One young lady, as she exited, impressed upon Williams that he must tell anyone who called up that she had to retire with a severe headache.

> *"Everybody?" he asked.*
> *"Yes, everybody," answered the girl.*
> *"Even the old gentleman?" he inquired with a puzzled frown.*

Answering the phone a moment later, Williams said about another girl, "Oh she has gone out with her fie-nance-aer."

This comedy sketch caught some of the flavor of life as it was experienced by many people in the Follies audience. As the *Times* reviewer said, "Nothing better fitting for Broadway ... has ever been inserted into a production built for Broadway." Williams, in this sketch, completely transcended the blackface caricature; interestingly enough, it was the only time he used his native West Indian accent on the stage.

Probably Williams' most famous scene was from the Follies of 1917, when he played a redcap working in Grand Central Station, especially proud of his son, whom he was putting through college. At the beginning of the skit, Williams bragged to the other porters of his son's genius and talent, and finally, when the son—Eddie Cantor in blackface—appeared, an effeminate youth wearing glasses with broad white rims, Williams' embarrassment and the eloquent difference in personalities between the two comedians, stopped the show. But

Eddie Cantor and Bert Williams, who were Sonny and Papsy on the stage and off, 1917

these moments of greatness were infrequent and fleeting. Much more common were the hackneyed "travesties" of *Othello* or *Sheherazade* that were only sporadically funny. Or the standard "jungle" routines, in the course of which, after someone called a lion "Leo," Williams muttered, "My God, a Jew lion!"

Williams was further hampered by having to work before the curtain while sets were being changed backstage. The unavoidable noises as backdrops were lowered and raised, and properties arranged, often reached the audience and diverted attention from Williams' stories and songs. As Ring Lardner once commented,

> *The people who wrote the Williams and Walker show knew how to write for Bert—the Follies people didn't. And he was under the impression, the delusion, that Follies audiences were drawn by scenery and legs and didn't want to laugh. He used to say, "I'm just out there to give the gals time to change." If you'd seen him just dance in the old days, you'd have pronounced him both "comedian" and "clown" as well as the champion eccentric "hoofer" of all time. But to judge Bert by Bert in the Follies! Well sir, you might as well judge Babe Ruth's pitching on his 1920-21 showing with the Yankees.*

In an effort to augment the Follies skits, Williams collected a number of stories and jokes from Negro sources, telling these humorous anecdotes as a sort of monologue between songs. Alex Rogers, who had written some of the best Williams and Walker material, collected these stories for Williams into a jokebook which has been preserved in the New York Schomberg Collection. These stories were told in Bert's Negro dialect and were primarily about unsophisticated or rural characters. Two of the jokes give an idea of Williams' humor.

> *"Has you got any ancestus, Mrs. Tably?"*
> *"Any whut?"*
> *"Ancestus."*
> *"What's dem?"*
> *"Why, people whut you sprung frum."*
> *"Lemme tell you sumpin', sis Twatley; I comes from rale, sho nuff pu' Afrikin stock dat don't spring frum nobody—day springs at 'em."*

*   *   *

> *The family Susie cooked for moved out to the Pacific Coast to live. They took Susie with them. After they had been there some months she said to her Madam:*

> *"I don't spec I'm goin' to be able to stay out here, Miss Em'ly, ain't de same. They's mo' like de Hawaiians or de Indians an' you see I'se always ben used to de puah Angle Saxon type."*

From 1914 to 1919, no other variety bill in New York offered Ziegfeld's array of comedians. Ed Wynn and Eddie Cantor moved at top speed; maybe their jokes were silly but their humor was high spirited and skillful. W.C. Fields, perhaps the greatest of Ziegfeld's clowns, was malice personified on the stage. In the 1916 Follies he caricatured Teddy Roosevelt and Secretary of the Navy Josephus Daniels, the attack on the latter in the nature of a personal revenge. Daniels was the hero of the Prohibition forces for his order prohibiting the use of liquor in the Navy after July, 1914. Fields' first ambition was to be a juggler, but he was even better at pantomime than he was at juggling. Ziegfeld also hired the clown Nat Wills for a Follies appearance with Bert Williams. Wills played the part of a tramp, with a red nose, a slit mouth, a battered hat and baggy pants held together with a string; from his waist-string hung a tomato can, the most sacred of his possessions. Splendidly arrogant, his specialty was a tramp monolog recounting his glorious thirst.

The Follies skits, songs, and dances followed one another at such a rapid clip that the effect of the show to Edmund Wilson was "the expression of nervous intensity to the tune of harsh and complicated harmonies." Williams' relaxed songs and stories, like Will Rogers' deliberate slow drawl, appeared a decided contrast to the "Anglo-Saxon straightness—straight backs, straight brows, straight noses . . . and efficiency of mechanical movement" of the Follies' girls. But everybody in the cast raced along, and Bert Williams had to keep in step.

Like other leading comedians, Williams also flirted with the movies. In 1914 he posed for a few one reelers, but the big projects that he hoped he might do on the screen were never realized. Williams went up to the Biograph Film Studios in the Bronx to make his four or five short, one-reel films. These were then offered to "the trade," but according to Henry Herzbrun, the attorney for Biograph, "All the representative releasing concerns were approached and they were unanimous in their decision that the Southern territory would resent and would not exhibit the pictures of a Negro star; they were also unanimous in regretting that this was so."

Williams intended to film all his best stories and scenes, and it is particularly unfortunate that he was discouraged from filming more of his great pantomimes, for the major part of his effect on stage depended on his visual appearance. Although his films apparently did not circulate, a one-reeler was resurrected and shown on television in 1961, and it clearly showed Williams' talent in pantomime. But the subject of the film is disappointing, and the mainstay of its humor is dependent on traditional racial caricatures. A group of Negroes holding illicit poker games in the back room of a saloon are the victims of a surprise police raid. Williams, along with the other gamblers, is taken in the police wagon to jail, and alone in his cell he acts out the famous imaginary poker game pantomime. In the company of the other gamblers in the back of the saloon, Williams' performance exhibits the full range of "coon" action; for example, at one point he cheats by taking a card from between the toes of a player who is using his bare foot to pass a card under the table surreptitiously. Nevertheless, the film does express besides the "Uncle Tom" clowning Williams' style and assurance, for in the midst of the blackface cavorting his poker game pantomime alone in jail is brilliantly conceived. But it is unfortunate that Williams, with all his prestige, consented to appear in the degrading sketches. On a Labor Day, 1963, television program devoted to the Civil Rights Movement in America, a clip of a second Bert Williams film was shown briefly, Williams in the role of a cringing blackface preacher paralyzed with superstitious fear in a "haunted" graveyard. The film clip was used by reporter Chet Huntley as an example of one of the most objectionable kinds of Negro caricatures.

Williams' phonograph records, more numerous than his films, give a more extensive view of his abilities. Under contract to Columbia Records from 1914 to 1918, he cut seventeen titles during these years, and as a recording star, he was considered one of the finest. An advertisement in the *Age* proclaimed:

> *Bert Williams, Caruso, Tetrazzini*
> *and other world famous artists can be heard*
> *in your own home*
> *by getting a*
>
> ### TONE — A — PHONE
>
> *The latest and cheapest high-class phono-*
> *graph made.*
>
> #### $10.00
>
> *Guaranteed to equal any $25.00 machine*
> *Will Play All Disc Records.*

Most of Bert's records were simple parodies of conventional stage humor of the period—for example, "You Can't Get Away From It" and "No Place Like Home"—but there were moments, like in "O, Death, Where Is Thy Sting?," when his drooping, deep voice would take on a genuine pathos and expressiveness. The recordings also give considerable insight into his vocal techniques, since most of them sold so well that it was necessary for him to re-record them some months after the first sessions. The later recordings often show a fresh interpretation of the material. Words have been added, an expression of the voice slightly changed, the rhythm altered. It is probably true that he never sang anything the same way twice, allowing himself a certain flexibility to adjust to his audience.

Like most great comedians, Williams also dreamed of appearing in more serious productions. He hoped one day "to stop doing piffle, and interpret the *real* Negro on the stage." He thought about presenting the tragic elements of human character, and talked over his ideas with his wife, but so long as he remained with the Follies, there seemed little opportunity beyond comedy and light songs. It was therefore with great excitement that he received a letter from David Belasco, the theatrical impresario, inviting him to Belasco's office to discuss the possibilities of leaving the Follies. Williams was so astonished at the invitation that he told a friend that he probably "wouldn't go at all, just taking up the man's time." It was only after the comedian was finally persuaded that Belasco didn't give appointments lightly, that he decided to make the call. Dressed in a new suit of clothes for the interview, Williams went in a taxi to Belasco's office, but as he stepped out of the car, the door handle caught on his new suit and tore a pocket of the coat. Williams, describing the incident afterwards, revealed an almost neurotic modesty. "You know—me visiting Belasco. All dressed up. So warm now, I had to tear the suit to get back to earth. As I tore it I stood on the pavement and said to myself, out loud—'That's the ape part, tearing its clothes.'"

In Belasco's office, the impresario shook Bert's hand, saying, "I have sent for you because you are ready for me." Belasco outlined his plans to present him in a play "in the not far distant future." There was no suitable play at the moment, it seemed, but he promised he would find something or write one himself. Although flattered by the offer, Williams never appeared in a Belasco production. Partly through loyalty to Ziegfeld, but mostly through apprehension about his chances for success in a serious drama, Bert gave as an excuse that he was still under contract to Ziegfeld. Belasco himself thought the comedian had been "overcome by diffidence and modesty."

Williams' extreme reticence was familiar to the Follies performers. W. C. Fields, who worked with him in two shows, was one of the few people to whom Williams talked at any length. Bert nicknamed Fields "Pops" because his blond hair was so thick that he resembled a character in a popular comic strip. The conversation between Fields and Williams that Fields later remembered most vividly occurred in 1919 during the Actors' Equity strike.

Bert Williams was the funniest man I ever saw and the saddest man I ever knew. I often wonder whether other people sensed what I did in him—that deep undercurrent of pathos.

My good friend, Bert Williams, met with a great many unpleasantly limiting conditions and as time went on he seemed to feel that craving for a club, or some place where he could meet those of his own profession, and talk shop as other actor-folk do. With all his philosophy, and he had a well grounded philosophy, he would occasionally say, "Well, there is no way for me to know this or that thing, which you say is going on—I'm just relegated—I don't belong." It was not said in a bitter tone, but it did sound sadly hopeless and it did seem a pity that any artist who contributed so much that was of the best to our theater, should be denied even the common comforts of living, when on the road in cities like St. Louis and Cincinatti.

At the time of the actor's strike, when Equity had called us all out and our theater had been dark about a week, I went over to the headquarters of Equity, and failing to see Bert's name on the list, I made inquiries and found, much to my surprise, that he was not a member. Before that time, I naturally assumed that he was a member, but it seems that he had not even been approached.

I asked the council if they would welcome Williams into Equity if he came and they were emphatic in affirming that they would.

I made up my mind to be very sure about this before speaking to Bert, because he was such a super-sensitive soul, that I would not mention Equity to him unless I knew that everything was all set right for him. I left Equity and went to see Williams.

*He was at home and glad to see me. I told him Equity wanted him.
He was pleased and grateful, but he was so sad and wistful. He said,
"Do you know what happened to me on the night of the strike, Pops?
I went to the theater as usual, made up and dressed. Then I came out
of my dressing room and found the stage deserted and dark, the big
auditorium empty and the strike on. I knew nothing of it: I had not
been told. You see, I just didn't belong. So then I went back to my
dressing room, washed up, dressed, and went up on the roof. It all
seemed like a nightmare.*

*"There on the roof stood the manager talking with a small group of
men. He went to me and said, 'Well Bert, are you with us or against
us?' I said 'Do you want me with you?' Then I went home. Here in
my own home, I felt more an outsider than ever. I couldn't feel that
I belonged any place. I went into the library and closed the door, but
I was not in a reading mood and I asked myself if I had any views on
Equity, pro and con. I had.*

*"Then I arranged some chairs in a semi-circle and held a meeting. I
started the Bert Williams Equity. I was all the officers and all the
members of both sides. I thrashed out the subject in true parliamen-
tary order. First I was the president and opened the meeting, then I
was each succeeding officer and I made speeches—anyway I had my
own little equity and that is what I called it. I held briefs for both
sides, because you see, I don't belong to either side. Nobody really
wants me."*

*I thought, said Mr. Fields, it was one of the saddest things I ever lis-
tened to and I felt ashamed that such a thing could happen to so fine
an artist. He thanked me sincerely for going to the front for him,
when I found that he was not a member, and he did join the Actors'
Equity Association on August 3, 1920.*

Williams never stopped encountering racial prejudice, but only rarely did
his impatience break through. Eddie Cantor told the story of Bert in a St. Louis
bar, ordering gin from a bartender reluctant to serve a Negro. The man behind
the counter frowned at Williams and said, "I'll give you gin, but it's $50 a glass."

Without hesitation Bert took out his wallet and produced a $500 bill.
"Give me ten of them," he said.

Although at the top of his profession, earning a greater yearly salary than
the President of the United States, Williams faced the same prejudice encountered by any colored man in the country. Social attitudes toward racial discrimination changed slowly, and while the First World War hastened the process
of integration in some situations, it did not bring the significant changes many
people hoped for. On a hot day at the end of July, 1917, nearly ten thousand
Negroes marched down Fifth Avenue in Manhattan in a show of protest against
recent lynchings in Waco, Memphis, and East St. Louis. Mayor Mitchell of New

York even closed Fifth Avenue to traffic for the afternoon, cooperating with the wishes of the demonstrators. The *Age* reported they marched "without uttering one word or making a single gesticulation, and protested in respectful silence against the reign of mob law, segregation, 'Jim Crowism' and many other indignities to which the race is unnecessarily subjected in the United States." Keeping step to the heavily muffled drum beats, the marchers carried inscribed banners:

— *Make America Safe for Democracy*
— *America Has Lynched without Trial 2,867 Negroes in 51 Years
         and Not a Single Murderer Has Suffered*
— *Were We the First in France? Ask Pershing.*

Bert Williams didn't march in the parade. Perhaps he was afraid a demonstration would have jeopardized his career, but more probably he was deterred by his usual diffidence, perhaps even a feeling of alienation as a West Indian. Except for a few benefits and the Frogs organization, he never took part in anything besides his stage performances. With his personal endorsement and financial support he might have helped movements led by men like W.E.B. DuBois or Booker T. Washington, who were spending their lives working for racial equality. But Williams never participated. Once discussing his attitudes about social inequality with Lester Walton of the *Age,* Williams said,

> *Since I have been with the Follies of 1910, I am more and more convinced that each member of the race must take it upon himself to solve the Negro question. I believe that the Negro is bound to get on top eventually, but it will be by pursuing a conservative policy.*

And Lester Walton sympathetically observed in his column about his friend Bert Williams: "The public is not interested in the race issue when it goes to the theater to while away a few hours."

Bert Williams, pronounced the greatest Comedian of the Negro race, was more closely identified with one song than any other. That song was "Nobody." His droll, inimitable humor, was never better fitted than by the haunting melody written by himself and the highly humorous lyrics by Alex Rogers.

NOBODY

Words by
ALEX ROGERS

Music by
BERT A. WILLIAMS

Moderato

Allegretto — (*Slowly* - and with mock solemnity)

1. When life seems full of
2. When sum-mer comes all
3. When I try hard, and

Till Ready — *p ben sostenuto*

clouds and rain, And I am filled with naught but pain, Who
cool and clear, And friends they see me draw-ing near, Who
scheme and plan, To look as good as e'er I can, Who

soothes my thump-ing, bump-ing brain?— *Spoken* (Nobody! When
says "Come in and have a beer?" — *Spoken* (Nobody! I
says "Look at that hand-some man?"— (Nobody! When

con espr.

win-ter comes with snow and sleet, And me with hun-ger and cold feet, Who
had a steak some time a-go, With sauce I sprink-led it all Oh! Who
all day long things go a-miss, And I go home to find some bliss, Who

p

says "Here's two-bits, go and eat?"— (Nobody!
said "That sauce is Ta-bas-co?"—*Spoken* (Nobody!
hands to me a glow-ing kiss?— (Nobody!

CHORUS *Slowly*

I _____ ain't nev-er done noth-in' to No - bod - y;

I _____ ain't nev-er got noth-in' from No - bod - y, no time:

And _____ un-til I get some-thin' from some - bod - y, some-time, I

don't _____ in-tend to do noth-in' for No - bod-y _____ no _ time. _ *D.S.*

HUMOR THAT MADE HUMANS OF US ALL

THE PUBLIC might not have been interested in the race issue, but Bert Williams had been neatly pigeon-holed by it. He was one of the first Negro performers to win the unqualified admiration of white audiences, but despite his personal success, he remained an unhappy, unsatisfied man, caught in the dilemma of being an entertainer whose talent and dreams transcended the theatrical personality immutably fixed on him by his time. In the eyes of his public, he was one of the most brilliant clowns who ever appeared on the American popular stage; in his own eyes, he was a failure. Bert Williams was a man who hated the stigma of his color, but the only way he had found to succeed in the theater was by wearing the minstrel show mask of burnt cork. He had struggled and worked to perfect his great gifts as a comedian, but he was expected to appear in blackface, and the role became as impossible to abandon as his own shadow.

Bert knew he would never escape the color of his skin, but the demands of his blackface role, as well as continual personal encounters with racial prejudice, were beginning to take their toll. It was only in private that he discussed the matter, as in a letter to a friend in 1922.

> I was thinking about all the honors that are showered on me in the theater, how everyone wishes to shake my hand or get an autograph, a real hero you'd naturally think. However, when I reach a hotel, I am refused permission to ride on the passenger elevator, I cannot enter the dining room for my meals, and am Jim Crowed generally. But I am not complaining, particularly since I know this to be an unbelievable custom. I am just wondering. I would like to know when (my prediction) the ultimate changes come, if the new human beings will believe such persons as I am writing about actually lived?

Taking a larger view, Bert got a certain comfort from quoting a passage from Aristotle, which he found reading late in his home after a Follies show:

> Is there any such happiness as for a man's mind to be raised above the confusion of things where he may have the prospect of the order of nature and error of man?

138

Often Bert dealt with the unpleasant situation by gently mocking his audience. A favorite entertainer at white society parties, Bert appeared in full dress clothes to start the evening, his deep baritone voice delivering his standard party remark, "Is we all good niggers here?" He was inescapably caught within the tangle of racial prejudice, and he was wearily resigned to the knowledge that social equality would not occur during his lifetime.

The tension arising from the incongruities of his professional life and his personal attitudes had its effect on his health, however. More and more often to get through the long hours of insomnia he left his home and walked across the street to Matheney's Cafe, to play cards, talk, and drink with a crowd of singers, dancers, actors, and musicians until dawn. Men who knew him recall that he drank heavily but always quietly, only with friends, and never lost control of himself or missed a stage performance. Always dignified and restrained, no personal scandal or public outcry ever touched his name. Only once, after hours of steady drinking, it looked as if Bert would be unable to perform, but he made it to the theater and got through his routine, drawling confidentially to the audience as he left the stage, "Excuse me. I don' feel quite up to it today. I ate some cabbage for my dinner, and cabbage jus' don' agree with me."

Although Williams had lived in America since he was ten years old, his strong identification with his West Indian birthplace meant that he never felt completely comfortable with his neighbors in Harlem, and he was denied companionship and support from people of his own race. He hired a West Indian chauffeur to take him to the theater, insisting that cafes lowering the color bar to serve him, must also serve his driver. Williams was in a constant state of exile: from the white culture, from which he was barred because he was a Negro; and from his Harlem neighbors and theatrical acquaintances, because he remained at heart a West Indian. He lived quietly with his wife and his parents. He and Lottie had no children, but it was with children that he seemed most able to relax. He would walk slowly along Seventh Avenue on sunny afternoons and watch them playing. They would gather around him and he told them stories, sang for them, imitated animal noises, and gave them rides in his Mercer automobile.

But as the years went on, Bert began to suffer an almost chronic depression. As W.C. Fields remembered, many such slights and unfortunate situations as the Equity strike episode, contributed to a state of mind which ultimately broke down Williams' health. He was a really sick man for two years, but bore up bravely in the face of everything.

Many people besides Fields had noticed that Williams seemed to be running down. For several seasons there had been rumors that he was about to leave the Follies, and in June, 1918, when the new 1918 Follies was having its pre-New York try-outs in Atlantic City, Williams wasn't in the show. He hadn't quarrelled with Ziegfeld; instead he announced he wasn't feeling well and wanted a short rest. But he couldn't stay still for very long. After only a few weeks at home, he got together some of his favorite old songs, and a new story—a ghost story built around the refrain, "We can't do nothin' until Martin comes." Ziegfeld had another show going on the roof of the New Amsterdam Theater, "The

Midnight Frolics," vaudeville acts to amuse New Yorkers during after-theater suppers. Williams' appearance in the Frolics was a surprise to audiences who had assumed his health was too poor for him to make such a quick return to the stage. He wasn't a well man at this point, but he couldn't rest. Congratulatory telegrams were sent to him from W.C. Fields, Harry Kelly, Frank Carter, Eddie Cantor, Gus Minton, Gene Barnett, Lester Walton, and Will Rogers (who was doing an imitation of Bert Williams in the 1918 Follies, wearing blackface and riding an automobile tire). When Williams stepped onto the stage at about 1 a.m. he received a steady five minutes of applause, sounding "like a barage and drumfire in one."

The ghost tale, "'Till Martin Comes," was one of Bert's most effective stories, and it is still vividly remembered by many people who saw Bert years ago. It was about a preacher lost on a dark and windy night, who knocked on the door of a farmhouse for shelter. The door opened mysteriously, for the house was apparently deserted, although full of furniture and with a bright fire burning in the fireplace. Going into the farmhouse, the preacher was surprised by a cat which came out of the fireplace and paused to eat the live coals. It was a little, friendly cat, and it was soon joined by another one, the second cat the size of a St. Bernard dog. It too dined on the coals and spit out the sparks, then asked, "When are we gwine to begin?" The first cat answered, "We can't do nothin' till Martin comes."

The third cat coming out of the fireplace was as large as a Shetland pony, and like the others, it ate the fire and inquired plaintively, "When are we gwine to begin?" The answer came in a chorus, "We can't do nothin' till Martin comes." It was at this point that the Negro preacher got up and said, "When Martin gits here, you tell him that I was here, but I'm gone!"

Heywood Broun thought this story was one of Williams' finest:

For all the humorous fantasy of incident and the whip-like finish, Bert Williams did not tell the story as a comic anecdote. By voice and pantomime, he lifted it to the stature of a true ghost story. We could see the old Negro, feverishly turning the pages of the Bible. The cats from the fireplace took form before our eyes. Sparks dripped from their jaws and the wind howled outside the cabin. All this was built for us by a tall man, his face clownishly blackened with burnt cork, who stood still, in the center of the stage and used no gesture which traveled more than six inches.

Although in poor health Williams continued in the Midnight Frolics through the summer. His chief physical trouble was poor circulation, especially in his feet, which became swollen and painful after the exertion of each night's performance. Finally, in October, 1918, he traveled to West Baden, Indiana, to enter a sanitorium conducted by "Waddy, the well known colored rubber and bath attendant, who is the only race man to conduct a sanitorium at West Baden." Williams stayed in the sanitorium under a doctor's care for more than two weeks. When he returned to New York, he told friends about an afternoon in Indiana when he was outside, riding his bicycle—prescribed exercise—along a country road. It was a new bicycle, property of the sanitorium, and Williams was rudely stopped when he was seen by the local sheriff. "Where'd ye steal it at?" the sheriff asked. Refusing to believe Bert's explanation, he confiscated the bicycle. The comedian walked back to Waddy's.

Williams had this humiliating encounter with prejudice only a month before one of his most triumphant appearances in vaudeville at the Palace Theater during the week of December 5, 1918. The dichotomy between his private and public life weighed heavily upon him after the West Baden trip, but he was a consummate performer, and once on the stage his inner melancholy only underlined his skill at causing laughter in the audience. Williams at the Palace always commanded a full house; people lined up from the box office to the end of the block, and usually "almost as many were turned away as there were in the theater." Reviewers commented on his "insinuating humor that gets in under the cuticle of each spectator, with artistry that made of each topical ditty a comic masterpiece. . . ."

Williams had signed with E.F. Albee of the United Booking Office to play in vaudeville on the Keith Circuit, as well as with Ziegfeld for the 1919 Midnight Frolics. With two shows in the afternoon and one appearance at the New Amsterdam Theater after midnight, Williams led a strenuous existence and had to enter the sanitorium again for a week in May, 1919. It was as though he were trying to lose himself in work. At home with Lottie he spent hours thinking up new ways to deliver his songs; she remembered that he "would sit quietly and smoke a cigaret, maybe two or three, one after the other until some idea way back in his brain had developed and then he would go to the piano and work it out, very quietly. His comedy scenes would develop in the same quiet way. He never ranted around and tried them out as we hear that so many actors do. He always proceeded about everything in home affairs or any other, in that gentle quiet way."

Williams appeared in his last Ziegfeld show, the Follies of 1919, with Eddie Cantor, Eddie Dowling, Ben Ali Haggin, Mary May, Phil Dwyer, Gus Van, Joe Schenck, Ray and Johnny Dooley, George LeMaire, and Marilyn Miller. Williams had a single spot in the second act which featured his songs, but after he asked Ziegfeld to let him appear in skits throughout the show, Ziegfeld arranged to give Williams more opportunity to act. The sketches involving Williams consisted of typical Follies humor, topical jokes and sophisticated innuendos. Act I, Episode 7 was called "The Popular Pests," taking place after-hours in a New York supper club; the cast read like the "Who's Who" of popular show business in 1919:

Waiter — *Eddie Dowling*
Janitor — *Bert Williams*
Motorman — *Gus Van*
Hat Check Boy — *Johnny Dooley*
Hall Boy — *Joe Schenck*
Taxi Driver — *Eddie Cantor*
Servant Girl — *Ray Dooley*

There is a photograph of the stars of the 1919 Follies lined up on the stage; Williams in blackface and black gloves, wearing a business suit and a checkered cap like the one on top of Joe Schenck's head. Williams' mouth, outlined sharply against the black make-up, is downcast, his eyes are wide and unhappy, his entire face mirroring despondency and dejection, in contrast to the smiling faces near him, especially Eddie Cantor's sly grimace beneath a ridiculous brush mustache. Despite the frenzy and artificiality of Ziegfeld's shows, the line-up of comedians suggests the talent and enthusiasm that the Follies used to offer its patrons.

If the glamour and the fun were sometimes frantic, Williams was remembered for his devotion and sincerity to his friends. He and Eddie Cantor frequently saw one another outside the theater. After their skit in 1917, when Williams played the redcap and Cantor his collegiate son, they called each other "Pappy" and "Sonny" off stage. Cantor has often told this story of Williams' thoughtfulness.

Williams had a splendid regard for every little feeling or emotion of his fellow man. He loved humor and even practical jokes to an extent, but when he knew that a practical joke was about to be played he always took care that it did not go too far. A very good illustration of this occurred when Williams and I were playing Buffalo together several years ago.

We were invited to take dinner together at the home of a mutual friend. And when we sat down at a table I found that the principal dish was pork chops. I never eat pork. Everyone laughed at me, and I asked if they could cook me some eggs. There were no eggs, so it be-

Johnny Dooley, Eddie Cantor, Gus Van, Bert Williams, Joe Schenck,
Eddie Dowling, and Ray Dooley, Follies of 1919

gan to look as though I would go without my dinner.

After some time the laughter died down somewhat and Bert turned toward the company at the table in his gentle way and asked, "Have all you boys had all the fun with poor Eddie that you want to?"

Everyone thought he had and then Williams turned to a servant. "Mary, go out in the hall and bring in the package you will find in my overcoat pocket," he said.

Mary returned in a few moments with a steak which Bert had brought for me without saying a word to anyone, knowing of the joke my friends were going to play on me. That was Bert Williams all over. He enjoyed fun and practical jokes but he didn't want anyone to go hungry because of them. That one act stamped him forever in my mind as that splendid thing—a true gentleman.

Williams was quick to help friends in unhappy or difficult situations, although he refused to associate with the "hangers-on" who frequently attach themselves to theatrical celebrities, and he discouraged a public image of himself as a generous man. Once Eubie Blake was with him in Matheney's Cafe when a shabby looking man was collecting money to help pay the costs of the funeral of a Negro musician who had recently died. Williams refused to give anything, but as soon as the man left the cafe, the comedian handed fifty dollars to the bartender, a trusted friend, with instructions to send the money anonymously to the musician's widow.

Nellie Revell, a white woman who was a press agent for Percy Williams when Bert played the Keith vaudeville circuit, was another recipient of a typical Bert Williams gesture. After Williams overheard the stage hands discussing a recent death in Miss Revell's family, he asked where she lived, then went to a florist and ordered flowers sent to her home. Miss Revell remembered:

When I returned to my home after the funeral, there was a large box of American beauties for me. I could find no card and the next day, I visited the florist and asked him why a card had been omitted. He said that no card had been left to go with the flowers. He could describe the man who bought them; he was a colored man with a fur collar on his overcoat—"I guess he was a servant of some friend of yours, Miss Revell," the tradesman said. At that moment I just knew that Bert Williams had ordered the flowers. The whole thing was typical of him.

When I arrived at the theater I went directly to Williams, who was waiting in the wings to go on. I did not ask him if he sent the flowers, but I said, "Why didn't you put your name on those beautiful flowers that you sent to me?"

He said, "Well now, little woman, if I'd been sure they would have reached you direct I would have done that, but I wasn't sure that they would and I didn't want to put you to the slightest embarrassment having to explain."

Although Ziegfeld had given him an unusually large part in the Follies of 1919, Williams didn't think the shows offered him enough of a starring role, so in 1920 he financed his own revue, the *Broadway Brevities,* written and produced by George LeMaire, who had worked with him in the Follies. LeMaire appeared in the *Brevities* as Bert's straight man, functioning in Walker's old role as a support to Williams' comedy. The new musical revue gave Bert an opportunity to perform in longer skits, and these comedy routines were interspersed between acts by "specialty people."

The origin of the funniest sketch in the *Brevities,* the "yalla shoes" scene, has been described by George LeMaire.

> *Most of us big heavy fellows suffer at times with our feet, and Bert was no exception. He would cling to one pair of shoes because they were "easy" and he'd wear them day after day rather than start out with a pair that were not so old, tried and true. One day while we were rehearsing, the subject of shoes came up and he said he had a closet full of shoes all standing in a row. He would take a look at them occasionally, close the door and put the same old ones on. This gave me the inspiration to write that scene which Bert and I did in the show in which he buys the new shoes and wears them out of the store.*

Audiences thought the "yalla shoes" scene was so hilarious that Eubie Blake had heard people talking about it for weeks before he was able to get to the theater to see it for himself. Williams, dressed in old clothes, ambled past some store windows and was attracted by a display of shoes. He started to go into the shop, but three times he nervously turned back, until he finally caught the clerk's eye.

"What can I do for you?" the clerk asked.

"I'd like a pair of yalla shoes," Williams answered hesitantly. With great care he accepted the bright new shoes, size fifteen, tried them on, nodded his head, and preened in the mirror. He threw his old shoes into a refuse barrel, paid for the "yalla shoes," and left the store.

After a half dozen pretty chorus girls had danced in the shoe store, Bert Williams reappeared, limping and disgusted. He painfully stepped over to the refuse barrel, rummaged for his scuffed shoes, and exchanged them for the "yalla" pair, which he dropped contemptuously into the barrel. With a blissful smile, he hugged his old shoes, and slowly exited—barefoot.

After turning down Belasco's offer to back him in a serious production, Williams appeared settled, at least for a time, in comedy. He told an interviewer, "One can't build up a character in a hurry . . . my job is to make 'em laugh and when they laugh I know it's going. If I were free to do as I liked, I would give both sides of the shiftless darky—the pathos as well as the fun. But the public knows me for certain things. If I attempt anything outside of those things I am not Bert Williams."

Having made a choice, Williams should not have been discouraged when on November 3, 1920, Charles Gilpin opened in a play called *The Emperor Jones* at the Provincetown Playhouse. This piece by the young dramatist Eugene O'Neill was destined to become one of the most important American plays starring a Negro tragedian. Gilpin was forty-two, three years younger than Bert Williams, and like Williams, he had wanted a life in the theater since his boyhood. In 1905-6, he was part of the male chorus in Williams and Walker's *Abyssinia,* but he was most interested in straight dramatic roles. After studying with Negro dramatic companies, the Pekin Stock Company in Chicago and later with the Lafayette Theater Company in Harlem, he finally, in December, 1919, appeared in the Broadway production of John Drinkwater's *Abraham Lincoln,* playing the part of the Negro clergyman William Custis. It was in this play that O'Neill saw him, and later contacted him for the part of Brutus Jones in *The Emperor Jones.*

Bert Williams saw Gilpin's Brutus Jones and admired the performance very much. Like all great comedians, Williams dreamed of playing in tragedy, but he had never taken any direction toward achieving this ambition. To close friends he might express a disappointment that he had never been associated with a great play, one that offered material to challenge his acting abilities, but publicly Williams told reporters that he hoped his own struggles on behalf of the Negro in the theater had "contributed something" toward Gilpin's success.

Probably Williams had contributed even more to making another show possible. A new musical revue called *Shuffle Along,* with an all-Negro cast, had opened in 1921 at Daly's Theater, on Broadway, and was to play there consecutively for three years, the longest run of any Negro show before *Green Pastures.* *Shuffle Along* presented a company of young Negro showpeople who had been growing up with the Jazz Age. They were not of Bert Williams' generation; their background had not been the dark years immediately after the Civil War and Reconstruction Period. Noble Sissle and Eubie Blake, Flournoy Miller and Aubrey Lyles, headed *Shuffle Along* with the talented young Florence Mills, who had learned her hit song, "Miss Hannah From Savannah," from Ada Overton Walker (Ada had sung it in *Sons of Ham* when Florence was a little girl). Featuring a hot jazz orchestra, the revue attracted crowds of New Yorkers eager to see a Negro show that had the fast pace and style of a Ziegfeld production.

Thinking back to twenty years before, when he and George Walker had been struggling to attract large crowds and to get into decent theaters with pioneer productions like *In Dahomey,* Williams could see that their efforts had not been in vain. Negro theater had come far by the 1920's, no longer so confined to the stereotype that had consumed all of Williams' thought and energy.

At the close of 1921, Bert's health began to fail rapidly. Lottie Williams would stand just inside the door of their home, waiting for the car which brought her husband from the theater. She remembered that "Sometimes Bert would have to hold on to the railing while he pulled himself up the front steps. The chauffeur would walk directly behind him. Williams was so sensitive he would not be helped up, because he did not want anyone to know how ill he was. Once inside the door he would sink into a chair even before he took off his overcoat."

Nevertheless, he rallied his strength for what was to be his last production, a comedy called *The Pink Slip*, written for him by Walter DeLeon, and produced by Al Woods. It went into rehearsal in January, 1922, but after an out-of-town try-out, it was renamed *Under the Bamboo Tree* and recast. Williams was the only Negro in the company, the members of which he called "my children." It was a weak play about a resort hotel porter (played by Williams) who was an outstanding prevaricator. Possessing a deed worth a significant sum of money, he decided to tear up the deed and sell bits of it to various people in the hotel, with the promise of great rewards for their participation in the intrigue. Predictably there were numerous complications and a love interest before everything was settled to universal happiness.

Before opening in New York under the Shubert's management, *Under the Bamboo Tree* was sent to Chicago for its first performance. In Chicago, Williams caught a cold which developed rapidly into pneumonia. He insisted upon carrying on with the show, but to gain sufficient strength he stayed in bed all of the time he wasn't needed at the theater. He was so exhausted after each performance that his stage manager and valet watched him day and night, dressing and undressing him; "the mere effort of moving enough to adjust his collar, tired and winded him, so that he had to rest between times, and the process of dressing took a very long time."

One afternoon Williams called his lawyer, Henry Herzbrun, to the hotel to help him write his will. When Herzbrun asked the comedian how he was feeling, Williams shrugged and said, "Bad stomach—but that's the way I am, feeling fine one day and not so good the next." Herzbrun asked him to close the show and take a vacation, but Bert laughed. "Throw a lot of people out of work? Never. I feel a lot better today."

To change the subject, Williams asked his lawyer if he'd read the debate in the *New Republic* between James M. Beck and Felix Frankfurter on the Mooney case. The lawyer hadn't seen the magazine, so Williams said, "I'm going to the theater in a minute, and there's a copy on the trunk. Read it and tell me what you think of it. And there are a few interesting thoughts about Mr. Taft as Chief Justice in the same issue." Herzbrun returned to Williams' hotel the following day, and he remembered that "We discussed the articles and talk followed concerning psychoanalysis, the movies, Gilpin, *Emperor Jones*, and other subjects. His political reactions were radical."

Finally, on Saturday, February 25, 1922, with both a matinee and evening performance to give, Williams collapsed half way through the evening show. He was, as usual, in blackface. A railroad car equipped with wheel chairs and blankets brought Williams back to his home in New York City. For a week he lay near death. Everything possible was done to help him fight the pneumonia, including a transfusion of blood from Will Vodery, and Williams at one point after the transfusion regained consciousness, murmuring, "I feel 80% better." But at 11:30 Saturday evening, March 4, 1922, he was dead.

Public reaction to his death was one of stunned surprise. Williams was only forty-seven years old when he died, and people expected him to go on making jokes for many more years. The New York *Age* chronicled the impressive funeral rites.

From last Sunday morning until Wednesday afternoon, people in every walk of life, irrespective of race, creed or color, paid homage to one who, during his life, helped to drive away dull care and worry with his original, quaint humor, always clean and at no time suggestive of ridicule.

From Sunday morning until Tuesday morning, the body lay in state at the Williams home. So great was the crush to view the remains that the police were assigned to the front of the home.

Tuesday morning at 10 o'clock the body was taken to St. Philip's Church in 134th Street. The family services were held there, and musical numbers were rendered by the choir. The metallic casket was covered with a blanket of white roses, orchids, and lilies, a floral offering from the widow.

Other floral pieces were from Eddie Cantor, The Frogs, members of Shuffle Along Company, Nora Bayes, Florenz Ziegfeld, and Miller and Lyles.

Bert Williams

When the body was carried from the church after the service the rain began to fall in torrents as if the heavens were weeping for the loss of so bright a star. Despite the downpour, the twenty honorary pall-bearers walked behind the hearse.

Two services were held at the Masonic Temple, 71 East 23 Street. From 12 to 1 o'clock, St. Cecile Lodge (white) held private services in accordance with an agreement entered into in 1920 with Lodge Waverly 597, Edinburgh, Scotland, in which Mr. Williams held life membership, to conduct the last rites over him.

The public services conducted by St. Cecile Lodge were most impressive. The Reverend Mr. Treder and officers and members of the Lodge wearing their white aprons, entered the room and formed a square around the casket. "Lamp in the West" was sung by the quartet of St. Cecile. A funeral oration by Dean Treder followed, after which the choir chanted the Lord's Prayer. The ceremony closed with the singing of "Still, Still with Thee." As the casket was being carried out of the Temple the orchestra played Chopin's "Funeral March."

It was the first time in history that the memory of a Negro has been so revered by white Masons of New York City. The Grand Lodge room was crowded to capacity, members of both races being present.

But perhaps even more touching than the public acclaim and ceremony was a scene in the Williams' home just before his body was taken to the Masonic rites. Lottie Williams had always disliked the gloves her husband wore on stage, because she thought he had beautiful, expressive hands. She forgot that part of the Masonic burial ceremony included a traditional pair of white gloves. When Williams was being laid out for burial, on the morning before the crowds were admitted to view the body, Lottie helped prepare the room in their home where he was lying. She arranged his hands so that they would be seen. Before her own death seven years later, she confided to her friends what happened.

Then the Masons came and added their rites. I saw the gloves. "Oh please," I said, "Don't put those gloves on him. Once—this last time, let his hands be seen." I didn't know, you see. He had to wear them.

CYLINDER RECORDS

BERT WILLIAMS ON PHONOGRAPH RECORDS

A. CYLINDERS (Courtesy of *Music Memories* Magazine, September 1962)

1904 It Wasn't His Turn To Laugh .... Co 200986
     Bill's Whistle.. Co 201030
     Bill's Whistle..Lambert 5176

1905 Bertie's In Love .... Edison 13166

1906 Nobody (2 minutes).. Co 33011
     I'm Tired of Eating in Restaurants (2 min.)... Co 32990
     Let It Alone (2 min.).. Co 33025
     He's A Cousin of Mine (2 min.) .... Co 33053
     Let It Alone (Obscure 6 min. cylinder).. Premier BC85086

B. DISC RECORDS (*International Discophile*—A Record Collectors' Guide, Spring 1956 and Spring 1960)

DISCOGRAPHY

MATRIX NO.		DATE MADE	LABEL
A-991-1	In My Castle On The River Nile	11 Oct 1901	Vi 991, Mon 991
A-992-1	The Phrenologist Coon	11 Oct 1901	Vi 992, Mon 992
A-993-1	Where Was Moses When The Light Went Out	11 Oct 1901	Vi 993, Mon 993
A-994-1	All Going Out And Nothing Coming In	11 Oct 1901	Vi 994, Mon 994

(NOTE: All the above were on 7" and 10" discs bearing identical catalog numbers.)

M-3615-2	The Ghost Of A Coon	8 Nov 1901	Mon 998
1083	The Fortune Telling Man	8 Nov 1901	Vi 1083, Mon 1083
1084	My Little Zulu Babe	8 Nov 1901	Vi 1084, Mon 1084
1085	She's Getting More Like The White Folks Every Day	8 Nov 1901	Vi 1085, Mon 1085
3616-1/2	If You Love Your Baby	8 Nov 1901	Vi 3616

(NOTE: Mon 998 and Vi 3616 were on 10" discs and the others on 7" and 10" discs.)

30038	I've Such A Funny Feeling When I Look At You	29 Sept 1906	Unissued
30039	All In, Out And Down	29 Sept 1906	Co 30039, A5031
32990	I'm Tired Of Eating In Restaurants	1906-1911	Co 32990, 3515, A298
33011	Nobody	1906-1911	Co 33011, 3423, A302
	Here It Comes Again	1906-1911	Co 3454
33025	Let It Alone	1906-1911	Co 33025, 3504, A305
			Co BC-85086
	Mississippi Stoker	1906-1911	Co 3557, A801
	I've Such A Funny Feeling When I Look At You	1906-1911	Co 3575
	Fare Thee! On Ma Way! Jes' Gone	1906-1911	Co 3593
33053	He's A Cousin Of Mine	1906-1911	Co 33053, 3536, A303
			Co A862
4682	I'll Lend You Anything	1906-1911	Co A915
4683	Something You Don't Expect	1906-1911	Co A929
4684	Constantly	1906-1911	Co A915
4849	Play That Barber-Shop Chord	1906-1911	Co A929
36538	You Can't Do Nothin'	Sept 1912	Co A6216
36539	How? Fried!	Sept 1912	Co A6216
38525	My Landlady	3 Jan 1913	Co A1289
38539	Woodman, Spare That Tree	7 Jan 1913	Co A1321
38540	Nobody	7 Jan 1913	Co A1289

(NOTE: 38540, Nobody, also issued in Audio Rarities LP Album No. LPA-2290.)

38553	Borrow From Me	13 Jan 1913	Co A1354
38554	On The Right Road	14 Jan 1913	Co A1354
38576	I Certainly Was Going Some	21 Jan 1913	Co A1321
39204	You Can't Get Away From It	4 Feb 1914	Co A1504
39205	The Darktown Poker Club	4 Feb 1914	Co A1504
45906	I'm Neutral	2 Aug 1915	Co A1817
45907	Everybody	2 Aug 1915	Co A1909
45911	Indoor Sports	4 Aug 1915	Co A1817
45925	Samuel	7 Aug 1915	Co A1909
45986	Hard Times	7 Sept 1915	Unissued
46004	Purpostus	9 Sept 1915	Co A1853

46005	Never Mo'..	9 Sept 1915	Co A1853
46006	'Eph Calls Up The Boss	9 Sept 1915	Unissued
46944	The Lee Family..	22 July 1916.........................	Co A2078
46945	I'm Gone Before I Go..	22 July 1916.........................	Co A2078
77341	No Place Like Home..	14 Sept 1917.......................	Co A2438
77344	Twenty Years..	14 Sept 1917.......................	Co A2438
78025	O Death, Where Is Thy Sting?.............................	26 Aug 1918	Co A2652, 35590
78030	You'll Find Old Dixieland In France....................	29 Aug 1918	Unissued
78031	When I Return	29 Aug 1918	Co A2652
78298	Oh, Lawdy...	13 Feb 1919	Co A2710
78299	Bring Back Those Wonderful Days	13 Feb 1919	Co A2710, 35591
78380	Everybody Wants A Key To My Cellar..................	4 April 1919	Co A2750, 35591
78394	It's Nobody's Business But My Own.....................	16 April 1919	Co A2750, 35593
78411	Elder Eatmore's Sermon On Generosity	29 April 1919	Unissued
49643	Elder Eatmore's Sermon On Generosity................	27 June 1919	Co A6141
49644	Elder Eatmore's Sermon On Throwing Stones......	27 June 1919	Co A6141
78828	I'm Sorry I Ain't Got It	24 Nov 1919	Co A2877
78833	Moon Shines On The Moonshine..........................	1 Dec 1919	Co A2849, 35590
78834	Checkers	2 Dec 1919	Co A2877
78835	Somebody...	2 Dec 1919	Co A2849
79126	Ten Little Bottles	18 April 1920	Co A2941
79127	Unlucky Blues	18 April 1920	Co A2941, 35592
79163	Lonesome Alimony Blues	6 May 1920	Co A2979
79164	Get Up	6 May 1920	Co A3305
79318	Save A Little Dram For Me	28 June 1920	Co A2979
79402	I Want To Know Where..	7 Sept 1920	Co A3305
79484	You Can't Trust Nobody.......................................	25 Oct 1920	Co A3589, 35593
79515	Eve Cost Adam Just One Bone..............................	12 Nov 1920	Co A3339
79516	You'll Never Need A Doctor No Mo'.....................	12 Nov 1920	Co A3339
79566	My Last Dollar	10 Dec 1920	Co A3356
79567	I'm Gonna Quit Saturday	10 Dec 1920	Co A3356
79934	Tain't No Disgrace To Run When You're Skeered.......	12 July 1921	Unissued
79940	I Ain't Afraid of Nuthin' Dat's Alive...................	13 July 1921	Unissued
80038	Brother Low Down	24 Oct 1921	Co A3508, 35592
80040	Unexpectedly	28 Oct 1921	Co A3508

(NOTE: 80039 is a master by Ted Lewis – Everybody Step – not Williams)

| 80191 | Not Lately.. | 24 Feb 1922 .... | Co A3589 |

The following master numbers are listed for reference only. The Williams recordings re-issued in the 1940's by Columbia were assigned new master numbers, thus:

78025	Co 27666	78833	Co 27667
78299	Co 27668	79127	Co 27661
78380	Co 27665	79484	Co 27662
78394	Co 27663	80038	Co 27664

All of the A5000 series recordings on Columbia are 12" discs while the rest of the "A" series are all 10" recordings. All the Columbia recordings listed without the prefix "A" are cylinder recordings.

DISCOGRAPHY OF BERT WILLIAMS & GEORGE WALKER

A-987	I Don't Like That Face You Wear	11 Oct 1901................	Vi 987, Mon 987
A-997-1	Good Morning Carrie	11 Oct 1901................	Vi 997, Mon 997
1086-1/2	My Little Zulu Babe..	11 Oct 1901................	Vi 1086, Mon 1086
	Pretty Desdemone..	1906-1908	Co 3410, Mon 3410
			RR V 210

GEORGE WALKER DISCOGRAPHY

995	Junie	11 Oct 1901	Vi 995, Mon 995
996	Good Afternoon, Mr. Jenkins	11 Oct 1901	Vi 996, Mon 996
997	Her Name's Miss Dinah Fair	11 Oct 1901	Vi 999, Mon 999

(NOTE: All of above except Pretty Desdemone are on 7" and 10" discs with same catalog nos.)

INDEX

INDEX